POETS TALKING

POETS TALKING

The 'Poet of the Month' Interviews from BBC Radio 3

by CLIVE WILMER

CARCANET

PR
611
W54

First published in 1994 by
Carcanet Press Limited
208-212 Corn Exchange Buildings
Manchester M4 3BQ

A CIP catalogue record for this book
is available from the British Library.
ISBN 1 85754 075 1

The publisher acknowledges financial assistance
from the Arts Council of England

Set in 10pt Sabon by Bryan Williamson, Frome, Somerset
Printed and bound in England by SRP Ltd, Exeter

Contents

Introduction

It was around 1962 that I first read a full-length book of contemporary verse. The volume in question was the Faber *Selected Poems* of Thom Gunn and Ted Hughes. I then went on to read *The New Poetry*, the famous Penguin anthology by A. Alvarez, which features the same two poets prominently. So the presence of Gunn and Hughes like magisterial book-ends at the start and finish of this collection of interviews gives it, for me, a certain symmetry, though one that was never planned. Certainly, when it was first suggested that I should conduct a series of interviews for BBC Radio 3, I expected that the Poet Laureate would at some stage be approached, in spite of his reputation for guarded privacy. And it is also true that my first list of proposed interviewees was headed by Thom Gunn, since his work has meant more to me than that of any of our contemporaries. But it is in the nature of broadcasting, like any sort of journalism, that one responds to the chances of the moment without much thought for the ultimate fate of the work one has in hand. In other words, the ordering is largely fortuitous and I have transcribed the interviews in the sequence of their broadcasting. And, of course, in the days when we were planning the series *Poet of the Month*, the thought of publication never crossed our minds.

The series began in the autumn of 1989 and ended in the spring of 1992. It was the third network's last attempt at a regular poetry feature. When I say 'last', I *hope* I do not mean 'final'. Despite recent fears about the future of cultural broadcasting, it does now seem as though Radio 3 will continue to be a broadly cultural network. Any reduction in that commitment would be a tragedy for the culture at large. This is especially true of poetry broadcasting. The third network's record in that field is an impressive one, which dates back to the creation of the Third Programme in 1946. It has had several distinguished poets and champions of poetry on its staff, Louis MacNeice being only the most famous of them, and it has commissioned as well as promoted new work of importance. However, the generalised commitment to the broadcasting of poetry, made when the network began, has always posed insoluble problems,* many of which also confronted me and Fiona McLean, the editor/producer with whom I mostly worked. One of the key questions was how to maintain a level of popular appeal without simply kow-towing to the literary establishment or to any particular version of what constituted the poetry of the day. It was also essential that, in focusing on current achievement, we should not lose sight of (on the one hand) the poetry of the past or (on the other) those writers of talent whose names on their own could never have pulled an audience. In the first case I think we deserve an honourable mention in the annals of literary broadcasting. In the second I cannot say the result was entirely glorious. At any rate, on both counts the *Poet of the Month* solutions were very different from those adopted by our predecessors.

In the period before *Poet of the Month* was launched, there had been something of a hiatus in the regular broadcasting of poetry. In 1987 the appointment of John Drummond as Controller of Radio 3 ended a period of more than twenty-five years in which poetry broadcasting on the network had been based around two programmes: *The Living Poet*, an occasional feature in which one contemporary writer would read and introduce his or her own poetry, and *Poetry Now*,† a monthly anthology of the air. I understand that *The Living Poet* has never strictly speaking died, though it has not been heard of in a very long time, but *Poetry Now* was effectively dropped when its last regular producer left the BBC. Originally the child of the poet George MacBeth when he was a full-time BBC producer, it was kept alive for many years by his successor, Fraser Steel, and then, for a brief phase, by Anthony Thwaite. By the late 1980s, however, though it continued to serve as a useful outlet for good new contemporary poems, it had lost much of its early vigour and was not providing a very noticeable platform. What was needed, perhaps, was a vehicle somewhere between the two established features, a regular programme that drew attention to new writing read by the poet and also allowed for some discussion of it. This, at any rate, was what emerged in 1989, when the Deputy Head of Features, Arts and Education, Tim Suter, and an arts producer of growing distinction, Fiona McLean, were asked to propose a replacement for *Poetry Now*.

---

* For a detailed account of poetry broadcasting from 1946 to 1970, see Kate Whitehead, *The Third Programme: A Literary History* (Oxford, 1989).

† Originally called *The Poet's Voice*.

They suggested that, instead of a single monthly magazine, a number of short programmes should be scattered through the month, all of them centred on a single writer. He or she would be interviewed early in the month – the model here was the evening arts interview *Third Ear*, also now sadly defunct – and would give a series of brief readings in the subsequent weeks. The readings would allow the poets to introduce, not only their own work, but the work of other poets they admired and wished to advocate; they might choose a poet from the past or an under-exposed contemporary or both. Thus Thom Gunn, as the first *Poet of the Month*, gave readings from both Walt Whitman and August Kleinzahler, a relatively young American whose vigorous, zany poems make you wonder why he is not better known. Eventually the programme settled down to a fixed pattern: a twenty-minute slot for the interview on the first Sunday of each month, followed by three weekly readings of about ten minutes each. The last of these was reserved for the work of the poet our monthly guest had chosen. (Some attempt was made in most of the interviews to touch on the work of the chosen poet or poets, which is why readers will find C.H. Sisson, for example, talking about Lucretius or Fleur Adcock about James K. Baxter and Edna St Vincent Millay.)

Once the proposal had been accepted, I was approached by Tim Suter as a possible interviewer and presenter. I was delighted to accept and fronted all of the first twelve programmes. After that, other presenters were introduced and my appearances became less frequent. I found it hard to argue with this decision. I tried not to be too dominated by my own tastes and enthusiasms but, of course, it was partly because I had tastes and enthusiasms that I was being used at all. To have a taste is logically to have a distaste as well and I accepted that writers I did not care for, or feared that I could not interview effectively, would have to be included. On one occasion, in a foolish attempt at neutrality, I interviewed a poet whose work I find simply dull. I still feel embarrassed when I think of the result.

When I was appointed I was asked to produce a list of poets I wished to interview. This was enthusiastically approved. The poets I named were as follows: Thom Gunn, Tony Harrison, C.H. Sisson, Czeslaw Milosz, Fleur Adcock, Geoffrey Hill, Donald Davie, Seamus Heaney, Christopher Middleton, Wendy Cope, Derek Walcott, E.J. Scovell, Jeremy Hooker, James Fenton, Elizabeth Jennings, John Heath-Stubbs, Stephen Romer, Edwin Morgan, George Mackay Brown and Ken Smith. I failed to net nine of these twenty, though some of them were tracked down by other presenters. I tried to mix poets to whose work I am passionately attached with poets from whom I expected some lively debate. I made sure there were stars of the literary firmament among them to offset some personal enthusiasms who are hardly household names. Eventually this provoked a slight dispute. I received word from above that there were not enough major reputations among the first few broadcast. We were told to think of our audience and focus on famous names. I still think that this was a wrong decision. Of course it is right to consider prospective listeners, but a serious arts network should surely make some attempt at leading public taste – as the network in question certainly does with music.

So the list of poets on the contents page of this book should not be understood as a personal hierarchy. I could wish that several poets were on it who are not, including some I had kept off my first proposal. Quite often the fact that a poet did not get interviewed was simply an effect of time and chance. On two occasions, however, I managed to arrange magazine interviews with poets to whose work I feel especially close but who would not have satisfied Radio 3 requirements. These were the American poet John Peck, whom I interviewed by post, and the Hungarian György Petri, whom I visited in Budapest. Since my conversations with them more or less followed the *Poet of the Month* format, I have stuck out my neck and included them with the rest.

When the journalist Gillian Reynolds was asked to review *Poet of the Month* for the *Daily Telegraph*, she phoned me up for some background information. She asked me what I most liked about my role as interviewer. Apparently I replied that I enjoyed being able to put 'the sort of questions conversationally that you don't ask in ordinary conversations'.* It has certainly been my experience that the informality of the interview can release insights into the creative process that critical analysis can rarely elicit. Perhaps it helped that I am myself a poet. I was naturally interested in things that don't normally strike the lay-person, even if he or she is a student of poetry. I am greatly engaged, for instance, by problems of form and prosody, so I asked about them as often as I could. These are matters not much discussed in the later twentieth century, yet to anyone who cares about poetry they should be as interesting as questions of theme and occasion, easier though those are to squeeze for agreeable juices. I

---

*   *Weekend Telegraph*, 1 September 1990.

also tend to regard the composition of poetry as a religious activity. By no means all of the interviewees would agree with me on that point, but questions deriving from my conviction usually elicited fascinating answers.

But the best of what emerged was unexpected. That, I suppose, is the point of an interview: if you know the answers already, there is not much point in asking most of the questions. What particularly struck me, though, was the way similar feelings and experiences emerged from very different people. Poet after poet explained, with varying degrees of patience, that the process of composition is inexplicable and largely involuntary. A great deal of what the poet acts on is unaccountably 'given'. For much the same reason, poets are often the last people to ask about the 'meaning' of what they write. Several interviewees – Adcock, Causley, Gunn, Heath-Stubbs – insist that what they mean by their poems is nothing more than what they say in them. Charles Causley puts it most neatly and sympathetically:

> I just wrote what I thought were very simple poems like 'The Nursery Rhyme of Innocence and Experience':
>
> > I had a silver penny
> > And an apricot tree
> > And I said to the sailor
> > On the white quay
>
> And I didn't really get worried until I started getting letters, particularly from America, saying, 'Dear Mr Causley, What did you mean when you said: "I had a silver penny"?' Well, I meant I had a silver penny!

I hope these interviews will increase the readers' enjoyment of the poems we discuss without sending them off in quest of 'explanations'. I hope, too, that they will enjoy the interviews for their own sake: for the distinctive tones of voice to be heard in them, for the passionate love of words these poets all have in common, and for the feeling – expressed by Tony Harrison, Ted Hughes and Michael Longley but shared (I would guess) by most of the interviewees – that poetry, even when it confronts our deepest terrors and despairs, even when it is widely disregarded, remains a source of hope for all humanity.

In preparing these transcripts for publication, it has often been necessary to modify the texts. Most people do not speak in smoothly continuous prose and this is as true of poets as it is of anyone else. I have only changed the texts in the interests of easy reading and clearer comprehension. I have never altered the interviewee's meaning and I have tried to preserve the character of each one's style of speech. In the case of the two poets who are not native English-speakers, I have corrected obvious linguistic errors and adjusted word order but have not attempted to modify the distinctively foreign flavour of their discourse. My own contributions have often been more brusquely treated, especially when the length of a question began to unbalance the interview. In most of the interviews I have made small cuts.

I should like to thank a number of individuals without whom either the programme or this book might never have come about. First of all, I should mention Tim Suter, whose idea the series was and who was responsible for my appointment. I am also grateful to Kathy Watson, who produced and edited three of the early programmes,* and to Simon Rae of *Poetry Please!*, who was one of my early advocates. I should like to thank my publisher Michael Schmidt for trusting me to produce a readable book before he had much evidence that it would be; he was also responsible for the publication of several interviews in the magazine *PN Review*. I could not have done without the skills of Fiona Anderson, who did most of the transcription, and Anna Janmaat, who agreed to help her out at the last minute. Most of all, however, I want to thank Fiona McLean, who is really the other author of this volume. She helped to create the series, proposed me as a suitable interviewer, and produced and edited the vast majority of the programmes. As an inexperienced broadcaster, I could have done nothing without her. I hope her contributions to *Poet of the Month* and to poetry broadcasting in general will be widely recognised.

CLIVE WILMER
Cambridge, 1994

---

*   C.H. Sisson, Stephen Romer and Fleur Adcock.

Thom Gunn

> I was myself, subject to no man's breath;
> My own commander was my enemy...

With those heroic words, Thom Gunn announced his arrival on the literary stage. They come from his first book, *Fighting Terms*, published when he was only 25. As things turned out, *Fighting Terms* was to be the last of Gunn's books written wholly in Britain. In the year of its publication, 1954, he went to California, where he has now lived for most of his life.

In 1989 Gunn celebrated his sixtieth birthday in San Francisco. Here was a major poet who, in living abroad for more than thirty years, had come to seem less central to British poetry than, to judge by his achievement, he deserved. It seemed a good idea for the *Poet of the Month* series to begin with an attempt to set the record straight. So we flew out to California to celebrate his birthday on the air.

Gunn is still the individualist of *Fighting Terms*, though the manner is now more relaxed and genial. In the late 1980s, however, a new need arose for the stoical disciplines of his younger self. The cause was the AIDS epidemic. As a homosexual living in San Francisco, he had found himself at the centre of a plague. In one month alone in 1988, he lost four of his friends. His elegiac record of such losses, now published in *The Man with Night Sweats* (1992), was beginning to be known at the time of this interview.

In the mid-1960s, the rather self-consciously heroic stance of the early books had given way to a gentler, more humanistic attitude in such books as *Touch* (1967) and *Moly* (1971). It is perhaps the union of this gentleness with the toughness learnt in youth that has made these recent elegies so impressive.

Your change in outlook during the 1960s was accompanied by technical changes: the development of syllabic verse in My Sad Captains, *for instance, and then of free verse in* Touch. *How did this come about?*

I started with a very limited kind of subject matter and a limited kind of voice, as maybe most people do. In my first book, *Fighting Terms*, I was trying to write heroic verse and I was influenced largely by the tragedies of Shakespeare and by Yeats; it was heroic in that sense. In my second book, *The Sense of Movement*, I got my heroes out of armour and on to motorcycles, so at least I got them into the twentieth century, but there was still a limitation. Then in my third book I started writing syllabics and, when you write in a new form, you certainly take on a new tone and you probably take on new kinds of subject matter as well. This allowed me to enter something much more relaxed, much less tense, something more colloquial. From syllabics to free verse was only a short distance.

This greater humanism, this greater geniality of feeling about life, reaches its high point with Moly, *which came out in 1971.*

Yes.

Those are the poems about the San Francisco culture of the late Sixties and early Seventies and LSD *is obviously an important element in that. After* Moly, *a kind of darkness comes into the poems. Were you conscious of that?*

I suppose so, yes. It wasn't deliberately decided on, it wasn't a strategy, but yes, I'm conscious of it when it happens and I'm conscious of it after it happens. *Moly* was a very happy book because taking drugs made me very happy. It's a book partly about dreams, whereas the next book, *Jack Straw's Castle*, has a nightmare sequence at its centre. I lifted the Furies direct from Dante.

But just the Inferno?

The *Inferno* as all poets have found is much more useable than the *Purgatorio* or the *Paradiso*.

The other thing that happens in Jack Straw's Castle *is that you allow yourself to write overtly homosexual poems for the first time. How did that come about? It must have been quite difficult.*

Part of maturing as a writer is being able to take more and more of experience into the meat for your poetry. To take an obvious and well-known example, take Shakespeare. He starts being able to write about limited kinds of subject matter: he starts writing certain formulae of the time. Then he gets more and more of life into his plays. Well, each of us, if we grow at all, does the same kind of thing in a smaller way. I started with just the heroic; then I managed to get more ordinary experience into my poetry; then with *Moly* I started to be able to write about the apparently visionary; and then about gay experience. Of course, Gay Liberation had a good deal to do with that. The fact that I'd made such a decision meant that I suddenly had a huge amount of extra subject matter I could write about in the next two books.

So it was a release to be able to write…

It was a tremendous release. You have to remember, if I'd started writing about this overtly in 1954, probably I wouldn't have been published. I mean it was that bad. I'm not sure I would have gone to prison for writing it. I wouldn't have got into America though. I don't think Faber and Faber would have been able to publish a book like *The Passages of Joy* in the mid-fifties. They would have been afraid of being prosecuted.

Since that book, a lot of poems have appeared in magazines which deal with the AIDS crisis. There's a whole series of poems – visions of death and elegies for friends – but so far these have only appeared in magazines and you haven't published a book since 1982. When are we going to see these poems collected?

I finished writing this book* in August 1988 but I'm not going to publish it until 1992. The reason for this is a decision I made some years ago that I was going to wait a specific length of time since my last book – I said ten years – because I have great difficulty in starting to write again when I finish a book. Last time it was about two-and-a-half years before I could write a poem. From the book before, it was about two years. So I thought I'd try to cheat it. As somebody said when I explained it to him, 'Oh, you're just playing a game then?' Yeah, I'm playing a game and I hope to win it! And I have indeed gone on writing – though I've been slowing down considerably this year, so maybe I'm not winning the game. It's something I'm trying anyway – I think a lot of people have this kind of trouble.

The book is going to be quite an event really, because it's not very often you get an experienced writer who finds himself at the centre of that kind of crisis. I wonder if you could talk a little about how those poems started to get written. Which was the first one and how did it come about?

---

* *The Man with Night Sweats*. In 1993 Gunn published his *Collected Poems*, which also includes the elegies.

I suppose I've always acted on the assumption that I want to be able to write about everything. I assumed I was going to live a good long time, since most people do live a good long time these days, and so I was training myself to write on as many different kinds of things as possible. I hadn't written much overtly about death because I hadn't experienced much death. My mother died early in my life but I didn't watch her die, and my father died in England while I was in America, so I didn't watch him die. So it's the first time I have watched people facing death and I've been watching a great many people facing death in different ways. This is one of the great old subjects, of course, but it's one that I hadn't ever touched on. The first one (I think) was 'Lament', which is the longest poem I've ever written. It's 114 lines. A friend of mine who had been living briefly in Arizona phoned me one day and said: 'Look, I have AIDS. I have to go either to New York or to San Francisco to get proper treatment, as I don't think I can get it here.' So I said: 'Well, come and stay with me.' And so he did come and stay. Two weeks later we took him into the emergency ward and two weeks after that he was dead. This was a very shaking experience – he was one of my best friends. He was the owner of that dog Yoko, by the way, that I wrote about in another poem. So I wrote 'Lament' to record this. Poetry has become one of the ways in which I deal with my life. It didn't start that way. I think probably I started writing poetry because I wanted to be famous, or some kind of rot like that. But now it is one of the ways in which I deal with things, in which I handle things. I wrote it in three weeks, which is a comparatively short time for me. It came out in couplets. I'm not quite sure why. I don't usually plan the form of a poem before I write it. When I write down the notes, I try to write them down all over the page, so that I'm not imposing a form on a poem that early. However, that's the way it came out.

Do you think that writing 'Lament' in couplets had some determining effect on the later elegies you've written?

I think that's a very good point. I think probably it did, yes. Once you do something that you're pleased with, it's not that you try to repeat it, but it points a way forward to other things.

One of the things that struck me is that you've had other friends die recently who didn't actually die of AIDS. I was thinking of Christopher Isherwood and Robert Duncan, about both of whom you've written elegiac poems. The poem about Duncan is in many ways a very traditional kind of elegy in a very English tradition of elegiac writing: one poet writing a lament for the death of another. It struck me that part of the power of the poem derived from our knowledge that, as you say in the poem itself, Duncan was a free-verse poet who even felt that he feared the idea of closure. Yet your poem is very distinctively closed in form: it's rhymed, it's in a very simple stanza pattern and all the rest of it.

When somebody complained to Turner that a painting of his was indistinct, he said: 'Indistinctness is my *forte*.' I think that kind of thing is my *forte*. I didn't plan things this way but it seems to be one of the things that I specialise in. Filtering some kind of subject matter through a form associated with its opposite. It's as though I'm taking street noises and turning them into a string quartet. I figure that, in that way, one finds out more about the street and one finds out more about the potentiality of the string quartet also. One finds out more about the rough and unformed and also about the elegance as well. I was aware of doing this in the Duncan poem and that, in a sense, is part of my subject matter in the Duncan poem. I'm writing about open poetry. In fact, the poem ends with an image I get from the Venerable Bede: the sparrow flying through the top of the feasting hall – in one open end and out the other – and of course 'open-endedness' is also the characteristic of Duncan's own poetry. I'm using that as a kind of pun.

The whole question of openness and closure is obviously something that is very important for you in the sense that you tend to move between one and the other. When you started writing, your manner was consciously disciplined and tight. You studied for a time under Yvor Winters, who's associated with that kind of writing. But over the years you've become more and more interested in a succession of poets who don't write in that manner – who, like Duncan, avoid closure. I suppose the first was William Carlos Williams, and then Pound, and then followers of theirs such as Basil Bunting and Duncan himself and Creeley. Are you very conscious of that as a choice you make when you write?

Yes. I'm aware of what I'm doing. I'm not sure how deliberate a choice it is when I first start writing a poem – I'm concentrating on the subject more than anything else, trying to get the individual words down. It's a very difficult thing to speak about. These are not just stylistic matters of course – the open and the closed – spontaneity and finish, the unfinished and the finished. I mean these are two things that occur at all points in one's life: you want to keep open to things but you don't want to keep so open to things that you're absolutely silly, that you're absolutely without any definition of your ideas at all. So you want to try to keep a balance between them at all times.

*You also seem to have got interested in earlier writers of free verse –
Walt Whitman, for instance. How long have you been interested in
him?*

I didn't really get that deeply interested in Whitman until fifteen
years ago, or something like that. I was reading the wonderful Penguin selection edited by Robert Creeley: really terrific – it has a wonderful introduction. I was on vacation in New York and I'd taken
this as holiday reading. I was reading a bit of 'Song of Myself' every
day, and I remember I came to part 52, the last part of it, and I came
to the line: 'If you want me again, look for me under your bootsoles'.
I thought that was such a terrific line, such great poetry, such unexpected poetry. It also sums up so much of the imagery of *Leaves of
Grass*, because what feeds grass of course is dirt: what you find under
your bootsoles. It's so witty at the same time, it contains so much…
I leapt up to my feet and showed it to this friend and said: 'Isn't this
great poetry?' Of course, I'd known some Whitman before then, I'd
read many of the anthologised pieces, but that was what really got
me on to him, really got me liking him a lot.

What about younger American poets?

Well, I admire a fairly new poet called Jim Powell very much. He's
just published a book called *It Was Fever that Made the World*
and what I admire about him particularly is that he combines the
extremely traditional with the experimental. I mean, one of his great
influences is Horace. Another influence is Robert Duncan. There's a
wonderful combination there! Another poet I admire tremendously,
who's extremely different from Powell, is August Kleinzahler, who's
just published his second book, *Earthquake Weather*. Kleinzahler
and I have an affinity, in that both of us are absorbed in the life of the
street. We're like cats at a window watching the constant movement
below. Also there's his gift for language, which is a very unusual kind
of gift. He says in his poem 'Earthquake Weather' that this crazy old
bag-lady – Mrs B. he calls her, he sees her on the street – is 'laying
down her stripe'. I follow what he means: it's like a human spoor, it's
her identity, it's perhaps a mental trail that she's laying down in the
same way as a stripe is painted in the centre of the road. Even the
phrasing seems familiar. It's like slang that I've heard somewhere but
can't quite place. But it isn't slang – it's all his and that's what I love
about his poetry. It's as if he's minting new slang and, when you
reflect that all language started as slang in the first place, you can see
that he's really getting into poetry one of the places that matter,
inventing language, making it new in that way.

It's interesting that you continue to like a good deal of the poetry you admired as a younger man. I know, for instance, that you're a great admirer of Edgar Bowers's new poetry, which couldn't contrast more than it does with August Kleinzahler.

Well, this connects with what I was saying before: that stylistic concerns are not limited to style of poetry only. They have to do with impulses and decisions in our lives in all aspects. Impulses, of their nature, are kind of open-ended and we have impulses all the time. We also make decisions all the time and those are closed, like closed lines in poetry, they're like metre, they're considered. Our lives are mixtures of those. So I continue to have sympathies with both kinds of poetry. I'm not surprised that I have sympathies with such a broad range of poetry: I'm surprised that everybody doesn't.

Does it strike you that we live in a rather confusing time with not that many exemplars around to guide younger poets along the way...

Oh, indeed, indeed. Being born in 1929, I grew up at a time when all the great Modernists were still alive and they were still flourishing when I was able to read them. Eliot, Pound, Williams, Marianne Moore, Stevens: they went on for quite a considerable time of my life. They mostly died in the Sixties, didn't they? It's very difficult to point to any poets of even comparable stature now. I don't think the poets of my generation have really proved to be very good examples to younger poets. Obviously the most famous and most accomplished poet of my generation was Philip Larkin. Larkin, however good he is, is set against rhetoric – rightly perhaps – and set against daring. Daring is just what young poets ought to be making use of when they're trying themselves out, when they're trying their wings in the first place. One of the troubles, I think, with British poetry right now is that the example of Larkin is holding people back. They should be imitating Bunting.

Do you think that what Larkin encourages is a fear of being pretentious – that it might actually do young poets good to be pretentious?

Yes, you've got to go through that. You've got to make your mistakes. Think of your mistakes in any aspect of life: how terrible to lead a youth without mistakes! You're going to learn nothing.

San Francisco, 6 August 1989
(Broadcast: 3 September 1989)

C.H. Sisson

'I have the greatest difficulty in believing in the existence of human personality, and I hardly know what sort of thing it would be, if it did exist.' With those words C.H. Sisson begins his autobiography *On the Look-out*: hardly a promising outlook on life for a lyric poet whose business, after all, is to write poems out of personal experience. Yet lyric poet is what Sisson is: one of the most searching and rhythmically compelling we now have. He discovered his talent for poetry late in life, the poems emerging gradually, like an underground current, from beneath a distinguished administrative career that took him to a senior post in the Ministry of Labour.

Sisson retired early, in 1972. Shortly afterwards, his collected poems and translations appeared: *In the Trojan Ditch*. Suddenly the landscape of post-war poetry began to look different. For one thing, unlike most of his younger contemporaries, Sisson had roots in the modern movement; and for another, very unfashionably, he is an Anglican and subscribes to Dr Johnson's definition of a Tory: 'One who adheres to the ancient constitution of the state, and the apostolical hierarchy of the Church of England.'

In retirement, Sisson has become a prolific man of letters. There have been several more collections of verse, many learned and astringently witty essays, and numerous volumes of translation: Lucretius, Virgil, Horace, Dante, Racine. As these names suggest, it is the past above all, history and tradition, that nourishes this impressive range of achievement.

One of your poems ends with the words, 'Only the past is true'. Could we begin by looking at your poetry in the light of that discovery?

Well, the future is imaginary, the present is happening and that only leaves the past to be true; and it leaves the past as, in a sense, all of a piece. Once a thing is done, it belongs to the past. When you write a poem, you write it in the context of the great poets of the past, not of whatever happens to be being reviewed at the moment.

I wonder if we could relate that to some of the things that you've been writing recently, * *because it seems to me that there's a kind of divergence into two kinds of poems in your work, particularly in recent work. For instance, you've got a new poem called 'The Pattern', which is a sort of long, semi-theological dissertation on the human condition in a manner that wouldn't have seemed strange to Jonathan Swift or somebody at the end of the seventeenth century. At the same time, a lot of your poetry and most of your method could easily be characterised as Modernist. 'The Usk', for instance, is distinctively in the Modernist tradition. Do you regard this contradiction as a problem?*

It's not really a contradiction from my point of view. You're quite right that I began with Pound and Eliot. That's to say, I was of an age that I got them, not from university teachers or from schools, but they hit me directly and changed my whole view of literature. My early poems naturally reflected this a little. But I gave up writing poems at the age of twenty – perhaps the wisest thing I ever did – really because I found the poems didn't satisfy me because they echoed either one or other of these two.

So how did traditional metric come back into your writing? Which poems brought it back in, so to speak?

Well, looking back on it, one can see that I gradually felt my way towards more complicated stanza forms. Of course, in the end one reaches a sort of near facility in these things, which has its own dangers. But I don't think the use of free verse or of a stanza form constitutes a real difference in the kind of poetry.

I was thinking that among the later poems in your collection In the Trojan Ditch *– poems like 'Martigues' and 'The Usk' and, to some extent, 'In Insula Avalonia' – there's something which I imagine you take from Pound: a kind of waking reverie, a dream-like association of images, rather than the sort of seventeenth-century argument I find in the poems you're writing at the moment.*

I don't think there's anything Poundian about it, if I may say so. I think, looking back on those poems and those times, they represent

---

* Most of these poems are now collected in *Antidotes* (1991). 'The Pattern' is in *What and Who* (1994).

an attempt to be plain about a state of mental confusion. Of course, one is always more or less confused mentally and in most other ways, but in 'In Insula Avalonia' for example, which, as you say, is only partly escaping from regularity, that was written towards the end of my official career when I was, without going into all the horrors of it, thoroughly fed-up with my position and uncertain quite what to do. This is reflected in the poem only to me; I don't think it matters to anybody else. It's clear that, in any particular period, one gets into one way of writing or another; I suppose there ought to be some rational explanation, but I'm not sure that there is. I mean, although one might think that, in a poem like 'The Usk', the fluidity of the verse and the rhythmic scheme give one a greater chance of introducing the unexpected, I have found that adopting a strict verse form, as I have in 'The Pattern', the mere certainty of the superficial way one's going leaves the mind extraordinarily free to produce what it wants to from wherever it produces it. I mean, I had no more sense of where I was going in writing 'The Pattern' than I had in writing 'The Usk'. In fact, I was astonished at the conclusion.

You do seem to have an ability to write in a way that seems continuous with a tradition that's two or three hundred years old, without artificiality and without in any sense seeming to be writing pastiche.

Yes, I certainly don't think of myself as imitating seventeenth-century poets when I do that kind of thing, but it is true that seventeenth-century poets have occupied an important place in my mind from a very early date. Even before Eliot and Pound burst on it, I was already reading Marvell, for example, Herbert, Vaughan, Traherne and so on. It seems to me there is a great naturalness in them, but I'm not talking about the language so much as naturalness in the way of thinking. It also ties up so intimately with the sort of England that I to some extent know at first hand, though in fact it's disappearing before one's eyes all the time.

Can you characterise this England at all?

It is imaginary, clearly, and it comes to me really from early holidays spent in Somerset on the Mendips. My poem 'Ellick Farm' is about the place I stayed in for a number of years. But, still more probably, it comes from my mother's background: her family were farmers in Wiltshire and Gloucestershire for generations, all the way back to the seventeenth century, so I belong there all right. I mean, I've walked over a lot of this country in times when one could walk over it and looked at the buildings and so on. It's nothing special, it's just that there are traces of it still there. It's characterised by, you know, the seventeenth-century manor houses, which make you realise that the gentry there – that's almost a term of abuse now – but they were in fact living very simple lives on the whole, much more like that of a farmer than we should think. Indeed, no farmer now would live as roughly as they lived. I suppose it all fits in the end round the person of George Herbert.

It seems to me that you have some feeling of continuity with the past which a lot of contemporary poets seem to feel that they've been denied. But the other side of the coin to that is, I feel, that you have a kind of impatience with the notion of modernism, if modernism is taken to mean something unprecedented about the condition of modern man. What do you think about that?

I think that man is much as he was and I think that man includes woman in that context, though I'm not allowed to put it like that nowadays! If you read your way into the past, you see how superficial are the differences. I mean, in recent years, a favourite form of reading of mine has been letters and memoirs. To take a famous example, if you read Madame de Sévigné from beginning to end, which I have actually done, you realise that there she is with exactly the sort of family changes and fortunes and relationships which are with us at present more or less – *mutatis mutandis*, which is plenty of course. One certainly can exaggerate greatly the changes of the past. I'm not seeking to pretend that nothing is new in the modern world. That's silly. But any fool can see that and it rather annoys me when people think they have to point it out – I'm well aware of that. Indeed, unlike many of the people who sometimes point it out, I've spent a working life dealing with people like employers and trade unionists and I have reason to know that the world exists.

What you were just saying reminds me of something that you point out in your introduction to your translation of Lucretius. You make the point that, in the nineteenth century, there was a tendency to pat Lucretius on the head as being extraordinarily up-to-date and almost worthy of being a modern man.

Yes, well it is extraordinary. He's always been thought to be on the side of enlightenment, and, in a sense, this was so: one of his great objectives was to discredit the religion of the ancient world and he writes honestly and indignantly about it. What I like about Lucretius basically is what I think Dryden said: he tells the reader nothing but what he thinks. There is this great directness about him, as indeed

there is about Dryden himself, and this applies not only to his denun-
ciation of the religion of his time, but to the whole tone of his philosophical enquiries. I mean, he is didactic. He is telling his patron
Memmius – whoever he may have been – all about the philosophy of
Epicurus, but in fact the tone is not that of somebody talking down
to a dumb pupil; it's very much someone who lives through discoveries
for himself and *must* communicate it to somebody. The result is we
have a great vividness in the descriptions of the curious atomic world
that he saw, or imagined was there, or deduced was there.

There's a point at the end of Book I of the De Rerum Natura *where
he's refuting the stoic doctrine that air and fire are centrifugal. If this
were so, he says (and I quote from your translation):*

> *...in a moment of time there would be nothing left*
> *But emptiness and imperceptible particles.*
> *For once you admit a place where matter is lacking,*
> *That place is the gates of death for everything*
> *And by them the whole creation will make its exit.*

I think that's a wonderful passage! There is behind it all this terribly
bleak view of the world, which is wonderfully presented I think in
those lines – as it is also in the final lines of the whole poem. There
are some ghastly scenes of the plague of Athens: the people lying
around, crawling in the hope of getting a little water and being
choked when they find it – really the sort of world people sometimes
imagine as coming after an atomic disaster.

*As you talk about it, and indeed as I read the poem, I have a suspicion
that there's a kind of identification going on here: I mean that you
feel something in common with Lucretius in spite of the obvious
differences.*

Yes, I did acquire, as I was doing the translation, a feeling of close-
ness to the author. This is something which one hopes to get in some
measure when one does a long translation, but it was rather a personal thing in the case of Lucretius. I suppose that modern element
in Lucretius does give one a sort of kinship – little though one may
be addicted to enlightened views!

*Of course, the enlightened views go hand in hand with a curious kind
of pleasure that he seems to take in the bleakness of reality.*

That's right.

Perhaps you might be said to have something of the same taste?

Well, I can see that this point might be made! But going back to Lucretius, the other thing I admire about him, which is very closely related to what I've been saying, is his brilliant sense of the visual world. There are all sorts of little pictures of contemporary reality: the flapping of a canvas over an arena, for example, a labourer trying to hold down a log of wood bobbing in the water, clouds tearing across the sky or great rivers rushing down. Lucretius does seem to receive directly from the visible world. The poor man is human, he can't stop there, he has to explain it, but of course the explanations are inadequate. They always are.

What you imply is that, in order to achieve a successful verse translation, you have to in some way identify with your author. Do you agree with that?

Yes, I think this does happen. It can be a dangerous identification. On the other hand, this is part of our *entrée* into the past, after all. There has to be a relationship between the translator and the translated. One does get closer to one's author that way than in any other way, and one gets close to him in a way which somebody not a poet himself cannot do, not with all the dictionaries in the world. Of course, one often gets told off by academics for not getting it right according to their lights. I did a lecture once on the poet and translator at the University of Exeter and I said there that it astonished me how people who had never written poems of their own would, faced with a classical text, suddenly think they could write English verse. Well, this is absurd, this is frankly absurd! The other pole of the thing is that, although a translator must expect to meet all kinds of reproaches from people who explain that the translation should have been otherwise, in the end the real satisfaction for him is that he may have written a reasonable book in English.

I think what you're saying about translation here is something that we might apply to attitudes to language and poetry across the board. There are so many people who talk about poetry, who see language as somehow a kind of plasticine that you can do what you like with.

It is absolutely the impossible approach from the poet's point of view. I mean, we're *all* the servants of language. One hears so much about personality and people, but these things matter so much less. The service a poet does is not to his blessed personality or to any other minor cause. It is to the language. It is what he has done in the end for the language, which is not an abstract thing: it is the invention of words that last.

I think this comes out in your work in a preoccupation with the nature of speech, the nature of the Word in the sense of the Logos, *the personal wording of casual opinion as against an attempt to say something fundamental about the human condition in the language of poetry. This opposition seems increasingly to dominate the work since about the time of* Exactions, *which was published in 1980.*

Certainly language is an increasing preoccupation. I believe less and less – and this may be just a symptom of old age – in the ability of one person to understand another or in one's own ability to find words which in any way capture what one sees in the world around one. And there are poems in which I go so far as to say one shouldn't be writing these poems because language is not up to it. But of course, it's all we have, and I would say that poetry is the nearest thing to human speech we have. That is to say, if human beings can marginally manage to speak to one another, they surely do that in great poetry as nowhere else.

London, 27 July 1989
(Broadcast: 1 October 1989)

Czeslaw Milosz

In 1980, after the first great Solidarity-led strike in Poland, a monument was erected in the Gdansk shipyards. It commemorates the workers shot by the police in an earlier confrontation. Inscribed on it are some lines by Czeslaw Milosz:

> Do not feel safe. The poet remembers.
> You can kill one, but another is born.
> The words are written down, the deed, the date.

In that same year Milosz was awarded the Nobel Prize for Literature. A deluge of publications followed: essays, novels, autobiographical writings, a literary history. But it was not until 1988 that a full *Collected Poems* appeared. In it, through the veil of verse translation, Milosz's greatness is unmistakable.

Half Lithuanian, half Polish, Milosz was born in 1911 and grew up on the borders of Poland, Lithuania and Russia. He worked for the Polish underground during the war, witnessed and survived the Warsaw uprising, served the Communist government of post-war Poland as a cultural attaché, and defected to the West in 1951.

For the past twenty years he's been Professor of Slavic Languages at Berkeley, where he lives on a lofty eminence overlooking the San Francisco Bay. I visited him there in 1989, just as Poland stood on the brink of its new democracy.

In your famous poem 'Dedication', which was written in Warsaw at the end of the war, you ask rhetorically:

> *What is poetry which does not save*
> *Nations or people?*

You seem there to be agreeing with writers like Tadeusz Rozewicz, whose response to the Holocaust was to create an anti-poetry. Yet there's a difference, isn't there?

You mention Rozewicz. I respect Rozewicz very much, but he belongs to what Polish critics have defined as a generation of 'the contaminated by death'. I guess I have been trying to overcome despair and, for that reason, I am not very pleased when critics try to keep me in that phase of my literary work.

Of course, your poetry is very different from Rozewicz's. There's almost a kind of richness in it, particularly in the later works.

Well, I guess I have been subjected to many influences, many more probably than Rozewicz. In the same year, 1945, I compiled an anthology of English poetry, not necessarily of my translations, but I gathered together translations of various poets, some of them very interesting. That was a sign of a slightly different attitude, a different orientation towards life.

Can you mention some of the poets you included in that anthology?

Oh, it began with the Metaphysical poets, and there were some songs from Shakespeare, for instance, and then it covered most of the history of English poetry. Among the poems which I liked very much in the anthology were translations from Alexander Pope, done around 1800!

You say somewhere that exile is the worst fate that may befall a poet. It doesn't seem to have turned out quite that way for you.

Yes, that was my conviction and I was of the opinion that I would destroy myself, but I had no choice. Or rather, it was a very tragic choice for me. But it turned out differently. I guess it all depends upon temperament – endurance, obstinacy...I used the maxim that exile is a poison: either it kills you or it makes you stronger.

Has it in any way made it more difficult to write in Polish? Has it made you want to write in English?

No. I have never had those problems and those doubts, which means that I was very deeply rooted in my poetry, not my language. I am technically able to write in French or English, but I have never tried to write poetry in either of those languages.

What becomes clearer in the poems that you've written here in California, I think, is that there's a kind of conflict in your work between what you want *to say and what you* have *to say. In your poem 'Incantation' you say of human reason: 'It puts what should be above things as they are'. Do you agree that there's a conflict?*

There's a permanent conflict – in the sense that I do not accept the world as it is. I have maybe mellowed with age, but basically I have always been a rebel against the world as it is in the name of a world as it should be. I am aware of all the dangers and traps along that path. In my youth I was a leftist and I know that innumerable crimes have been committed in the name of looking for a world as it should be. But this is something quite elementary, I think.

The issue of conflict seems to dominate your poetry in some way. For instance, you have an impulse to praise. I believe you translated the Psalms at some stage.

Yes. This is not the same conflict because my poetry is basically a poetry of praise. It's an affirmation of the world, of the beauty of the world and, at the same time, it's a protest against cruelty. I cannot accept the cruelty of the world, and in this respect there is maybe some similarity between myself and another Nobel laureate born in Poland, Isaac Bashevis Singer. So this is a basic problem of human existence: that you cannot live by pure negation and you cannot live by affirmation created in a fools' paradise.

But when you talk about the cruelty of the world, are you talking there primarily about the cruelty of the human world, I mean such as the political crimes that you were referring to...?

No, no. Ever since I was an adolescent, I have been very sensitive to biology – to what we learn from biology. I mean the whole world of live matter, suffering and cruelty. Cruelty, of course, not according to criteria inherent in nature, which is completely indifferent, but according to our human criteria.

So this accounts for what – in your book Native Realm *and in some of your poems – you call Manichaeism perhaps?*

Well, with the difference that Manichaeism was a heresy, and quite a potent heresy, for many centuries. It included the Albigensian heresy in the South of France. It exists today, not as we might create a Manichaean Church or an Albigensian religion, but as a sort of a permanent ingredient of our thinking about the world.

I wonder if we could talk a little bit now about an American poet whom I think you admire, and that's Walt Whitman. It seems to me that Whitman is a poet that one might not associate with you initially, in the sense that there is something almost of the innocent about him. But, of course, Whitman like you was an admirer of the

Psalms, and one can hardly think of anybody more addicted to praise in his poetry than he was.

I can tell you that my affinity with Whitman is real and, curious as it may sound, it goes back to Whitman's form of verse. Of course Whitman's verse is based upon the Bible, and the fact that I have translated the Psalms and translated the Bible shows my inclination, too, towards that form. In English the form is called Biblical verse, in French it is *le verset*. My first acquaintance with Whitman was a fascination with that form, which of course is not a form at all – it's connected with, I should say, an ecstatic element in Whitman and, of course, Whitman played a big role in the changes in versification in several European languages.

There are certain poems of yours – 'With Trumpets and Zithers', 'Throughout Our Lands' and 'Dithyramb' – which are clearly influenced by Whitman in their manner. Would it be true to say that the way you wrote in Polish was affected by Whitman's way of writing English or were there also Polish models?

Oh, undoubtedly, undoubtedly. This is a question of the qualities peculiar to languages. The Polish language is a language of weak accents and, for that reason, metre and rhyme have been abandoned in the modernist revolution of our century, largely abandoned, so there was a search for new formulas in versification. You know that from experience, because you mentioned Rozewicz, who also writes in non-metrical verse. Occasionally I write rhymed and metred poems, but that's with a touch of self-irony and humour. But Russian poetry, like the poetry of my friend Joseph Brodsky, is metrical and rhymed and that's due to the different laws of language, I should say.

Do you never envy Brodsky? Do you never feel a nostalgia for the old metres?

No, no. Because I feel that the laws of languages are completely different. I have to submit to the laws of my language.

I wonder if we could talk about another poet whom I know you admire and who also learned from Whitman, and that's the Californian poet Robinson Jeffers. You've written a wonderful poem about him, which is curiously ambivalent. It seems to be a sort of tribute, and yet…

Oh, yes. Yes, I have been engaged in a very intense quarrel with Jeffers for many years, for many years. Even at the time when Jeffers was practically forgotten – because there was such a period – I defended him as a very important poet. Now he seems to be back, as a poet who propagated respect for nature, so he comes back on, let us say, the ecological current. But my quarrel with him is still very real.

What's the nature of your quarrel with him?

I guess that he's a little too American for my taste. In him there are those old influences of science upon the American mind, beginning with Darwin and ending with Freud and Jung and Nietzsche. It seems to me that a poet who takes the impact of science upon our imagination too seriously creates a somewhat illusory world, because I am primarily concerned with the human world. The fact is that we cannot separate ourselves from the human world, as Jeffers tried to by creating his philosophy of so-called 'inhumanism'; we're submerged for better or worse in the human world. So we live in a microcosm of human things and, if you want to have a view of millions and millions of years of galaxies, stars, evolution and so on, you enter the realm of macro-vision. I'm not sure whether this is accessible to our modest human imagination.

So in your poem 'To Robinson Jeffers', when you talk about the old Slavic poets and towards the end you say,

> *Better to carve suns and moons on the joints of crosses*
> *as was done in my district,*

are you there setting the European world against...

Yes, I am setting the world of a small district with funny customs, superstitions...I have written a novel, you know, *The Issa Valley*, which is about such a district.

So it's a kind of intuitive humanism that one finds in the older civili- sations.

Well, it is probably also connected with Christianity, because Jeffers has been defined as trying to create a kind of new religion close to Buddhism but in a Western way and, of course, in that religion there is no place for reincarnation.

So it's inhuman.

Yes. So that's the worship of eternal nature as God.

It seems to me that there's another conflict in your work – or maybe at root it's the same conflict – which is that you mistrust the non-

human world but at the same time you have a passion for particulars. I'm thinking of a number of poems where there are moments of epiphany – eternal moments if you like – and these eternal moments seem to be set against history. Is that a conflict?

Yes, and here I should mention that after all, to a large extent, there are some mystical elements in my poetry. I mentioned my English influences, but I have had my share of French influences – among others, my late cousin Oscar Milosz. He was a French poet and a mystical writer, who died in 1939. So that line is very strong in my work.

Perhaps it would be interesting for you to comment on your relation to Christianity, which seems also curiously ambivalent. It's never clear to me to what extent you would be happy to call yourself a Christian.

Well, the Pope, who is a very good literary critic and who reads a lot of poetry in various languages, once said to me, talking about my poems: 'You seem to take a step forward and then a step back.' I said: 'Holy Father, is there any other way of writing religious poetry in the twentieth century?'

Do you now reach a bigger audience in English than you do even in Polish?

Oh, in Polish that's somewhat crazy because after the Nobel Prize I was defrozen completely, because until the Nobel Prize I was a non-person for a long time. People didn't know about my existence. They were furious to learn that the Nobel Prize had been won by a Polish poet they hadn't heard of! They criticised the government for that. So that was a bigger thing after I received the Nobel Prize. It lasted, however, until martial law, when I was put back into the freezer.

Were you available in samizdat *at that time?*

Oh, yes. Many of my books, in prose and in verse. I lost count because what was called 'parallel publishing', as you probably know, was a big business in Poland, so I don't know. But many books were published in that way.

I began by asking you a question which touched on the poet's role in society and, if you like, the responsibility of the poet. There's a famous line, for instance, of W.H. Auden's: 'Poetry makes nothing happen.' Do you think the poet has a role to play in these new developments in Poland?

For centuries Polish poetry has felt the impact of history and it's imbued with something which we call 'historicity'. For that reason, we have elaborated some very subtle relations between poet and community. It's not necessarily a poetry of direct commitment that participates in and influences a community. During martial law there were a great many protest poems, all very committed and so on, but I am not sure whether this is the way. During the war, for instance, I wrote some poems which were obviously political, but I don't think that this is the proper road for a poet to take, unless he is completely forced and cornered and has no way out. I accept that that voices his indignation. But there are many ways of maintaining what they call the 'farm' of a poetry in a given language, and so the relations between the state of society and poetry are subtle, multi-faceted, and always present.

Berkeley, California, 8 August 1989
(Broadcast: 2 November 1989)

Stephen Romer

'Of Comfort in Books' is a love-poem from Stephen Romer's first collection, *Idols*. In the poem, the speaker thinks of a cycle of love-poems by another poet, a writer of the French Renaissance. By the end of the poem he has become aware that his own relationship is somehow following the plot of the French cycle. He and the woman he loves are

stuck

> in somebody's *Amours* at chanson seven.
> From here to chanson twelve is hell to heaven
>
> but our game old poet seemed to work his miracle.
> Or was he lying, to finish the cycle?

This quietly ironic feeling for the way art and life, the real and the ideal, converge and diverge is typical of Romer. It makes for a poetry that surprises you with its originality while at the same time drawing heavily on tradition – on how the inescapable subjects (love and loss and separation) have been dealt with in the past.

Romer was born in 1957, studied at Cambridge and Harvard, and has lived in Paris since 1981. *Idols* was published in 1986, but I first came across his work in the early Eighties when he wrote a regular column on the French literary scene for *PN Review*. During the same period, he began translating contemporary French poets and produced an accomplished selection of Jacques Dupin, the most radically minimalist of the better-known figures. French poetry and the French language itself have left their mark on Stephen Romer's poetry, though he remains in some ways a very English sort of writer: to my mind the most interesting poet of his generation.

His new book, *Plato's Ladder*, was published in 1992.

Idols *is rather an enigmatic title. What did you mean by it?*

There are two types of idol in the book. There's the human idol, the idealised woman, and in the second part of the book there's an idol which is a phantasm of a religion, which is in fact a false religion because it falls into idolatry and not into what is on the other side of idolatry, the true transcendence beyond idolatry. There's a negative connotation in the title *Idols*, which is finally how idolising something completely dehumanises it. I'm reminded a lot – and I must have recalled – that there's a passage in Proust where Swann falls in love with his mistress Odette mainly because she reminds him of a painting by Botticelli and therefore out of her mobile human face he fixes an image. I think finally this is a dangerous or risky thing to do. I suppose I meant anything that sets itself up in the mind, that causes a tyranny in the mind and which one would dearly love to exorcise. My next book may well be called *Iconoclasms*!

A lot of the poems seem to proceed by a kind of imperfect analogy. The patterns in the mind that you talk about are very often derived from other disciplines of thought. There's a poem called 'Theory', which makes use of mathematics, and there's a poem about Héloïse and Abelard, which makes use of theology, and there's a poem called 'Grammar', which compares grammatical rules to the way things turn out in the actual structure of experience. You seem very often to be playing off a system of thought against a pattern of experience. Does this make you a philosophical poet?

That's an interesting question. I think somebody said that poetry provides the emotional equivalent of thought. When a poet dabbles in philosophy or metaphysics, he's concerned to work through a thesis emotionally. A premise such as solipsism, for instance: he's concerned to work that through emotionally, as if to say, 'Here's an interesting idea.' For example, in my poem 'Theory', in which I say every point of view is described by a circle: that is to say there is no objectivity, there is no possible mutual shared point of view – which is an interesting, evocative idea. It seems to me that the poet's job – or what I try to do – is to see how that feels on the pulses.

I feel there's a sort of paradox embodied in your poetry: on the one hand, it seems to be preoccupied in a very positive way with the absolute and, on the other, it seems to be very ironic about that. Is this an inconsistency?

It certainly may seem to be an inconsistency. Again, it's something

I feel pragmatically. Re-reading my work, I was struck precisely by how many times there is a persona in the poems who – whether frivolously or, in some, very seriously – is determined to change his life. In 'Higher Things', one of the poems which illustrates this, I have the lines: 'I shall need all his courage for the task / of settling firmly to the sublime.' That is to say, of casting out the human idol in favour of the absolute divine love. I think that that – even though I treat it flippantly or ironically in the love cycle of my poems – is a perennial theme and finally a very serious theme in my work.

You write in what one could call metre and you use what one would call rhyme, but you don't use them in ways that are conventional. There's a kind of deliberate inexactness. How did this method evolve and what do you see yourself as doing with it?

I think I developed the metre as flexibly as I could. I find the couplets which I use for the love poems absolutely suited to the kind of argumentative and gritty (I hope) philosophical discourse which ends almost with a clinching line or with a QED, but I've found the off-rhyme also added impetus to the movement of the poem, whereas a full rhyme would have been too heavy – although I use them on occasion. The syllables work within the framework of the iambic pentameter but much more freely.

Did you begin by writing in fairly conventional couplets and dis-cover ways of deviating from regularity, or was it the other way round?

I think it stemmed earlier from when I used to write sonnets, very regular sonnets in iambic pentameters. When I was at Harvard I did a prosody course with Robert Fitzgerald, which has always stood me in good stead, partly because I knew properly what a Catullan hen-decasyllable was or an iambic pentameter. He made us write poems in set verse-forms and I think the advantage of knowing that is that you then know how best to depart from the regular form.

Your combination of irony and mysticism and also your preoccupa-tion with ways of deviating from apparently regular metres: these are reminiscent of Pound and Eliot when they were working most closely together in the years just after the First World War. Have their poems of those years had an effect on you?

I can certainly see it as a comparison to be made. I would perhaps say that my poems are less deliberately satirical in mode. I think when Eliot and Pound wrote those quatrain poems they were deliberately setting up a new style against Georgianism. They were trying to inject some bite, particularly some French bite from Corbière or Laforgue or Gautier, into a very flaccid English poetry, as it then was. I'm particularly interested in Eliot's ironies – the ironic slippage you find in a poem like 'Portrait of a Lady', in which the attitudinising, posing, self-possessed young man suddenly finds his ironic pose deserting him. There's a moment in 'Portrait of a Lady' where he says: 'My self-possession gutters; we are really in the dark.' And also, at the end of that same poem, where the irony is actually subsumed by what seems to be a moral earnestness, where he imagines the lady dying and poses the plangent question: 'And should I have the right to smile?'

So in a way the ironic edge that you're talking about in Eliot conceals this deep, Romantic, emotional surge, which has to be somehow or other held down. Do you feel a similar tension in your own work?

Yes, definitely and I think for me, perhaps, my best poems are where the ironic mask slips. Maybe it unconsciously slips but the irony is certainly hiding a depth or an uncertainty: I think it's above all a defensive posture.

A poet I know you admire is the Victorian poet, Arthur Hugh Clough – I was just thinking of a line of his, which says: 'Utterly vain is, alas! this attempt at the Absolute, – wholly!'

Graham Greene called Clough one of the few adult poets in the nineteenth century and I think that's a very just appraisal of him. I'm attracted to him precisely because he takes ironic jabs all the time at the Victorian establishment, even though – and this is interesting about him – he was groomed to be the ideal pious Victorian. He's interesting also because his contemporaries regarded him as something of a failure, as someone who didn't fulfil his promise. *Amours de Voyage*, one of his greatest poems, drew the censure of such eminent Victorians as Emerson and Matthew Arnold because they couldn't accept a portrait of failure.

Claude in Amours de Voyage *is an English tourist in Rome and it's a classic tourist poem in some ways, isn't it?*

Yes it is. I mean it's full of the classic blasé ironies of the Englishman on the Grand Tour, who finds Rome disappointing, who finds it 'rubbishy': this was apparently a common conventional reaction to Rome. But it's not *just* a tourist poem, because it also takes place in the context of Mazzini and Garibaldi, who had just proclaimed the

Roman republic, which fell to the French in July 1849. Also, there's a love interest in the poem, the *amour de voyage*, which provides narrative and, finally, introspection. There are ample opportunities for irony in all these domains, but what I particularly like about the poem is how, at the end, the irony deserts Claude – ironic slippage again – and it turns into a very poignant contemplation of faith and love and knowledge.

And it has the same mixture of a curiously colloquial manner with a highly literary and literate mode of reference.

That's right. I think what is surprising, what is immediately attractive about Clough's poem, is its colloquial aspect. That's what immediately attracted me to it – something like: 'Am I prepared to lay down my life for the British female?' It has all the rhythm of colloquialism but also of stance, attitudinising and irony.

You've spent the best part of your creative life in France, haven't you? And you've translated a good deal of French poetry – not just Symbolist poetry, but modern poetry as well – Jacques Dupin, Yves Bonnefoy and so on. Do you now feel rather French?

I think it actually runs less deep than one might suppose. Maybe I'm wrong, but I don't feel they actually impinge so much on my own work. I think the French and English traditions are radically different. There's a particular post-Mallarméan reflexiveness and theory in French poetry that seems quite alien to the English temper. I think there was one Cambridge Poetry Festival in which a French poet proclaimed that an English poet's poem, which was a description of a garden, was simply not a poem because it didn't discuss itself rigorously enough.

Can you just elucidate what you mean by reflexiveness in this case?

Yes, I think reflexiveness turns out to mean a radical mistrust of language: fractured syntax, almost an inability to deal with the real world, or anything but the very archetypal or pure elements of the world. (The pre-Socratic philosophers have been very important to some modern French poets.) But I find there's a strangely deserted landscape in modern French poetry. I mean, there's a great deal of white space for one thing...

Whereas English poetry is full of material objects.

Exactly. I mean, you take a poem by Larkin – 'Here' or 'Church Going' or one of those poems where he has catalogues, lists of objects:

that is unthinkable in French poetry. In fact, I've had quite a lot of experience of translating with young French poets and, when they come to translate certain poems by contemporaries of mine, poems that contain such objects, they say: 'No this simply won't work in French. We cannot put headlights or boots or hair-dos or whatever it is in our poems.'

It seems to me that you have, nonetheless, a kind of French poetry in the background a lot of the time – indeed not just French poetry, but French culture. There are several poems in Idols *which are set in restaurants and cafés of an obviously Parisian kind, in which multiple mirrors occur, and it seems to me that the mirrors with their 're-flexiveness' almost introduce a bit of the French world of poetry into the English world of the poem.*

I think the French terrorists or theorists would protest against that as being perhaps too ludic, but certainly I like to think that one can apply reflexiveness. I think reflexiveness certainly is there in the sense of an exacerbated self-consciousness you get in Paris. Not only is the incidence of beauty extraordinary in that city, but it's only equalled by the incidence of vanity.

Do you think that your poetry is going to lead you further in the direction of the transcendental? I'm thinking of new poems like 'Plato's Ladder' and 'The Question'.

I wouldn't want to lose myself in the solemnity of the transcendental. I think that would be a dangerous move, and I hope 'Plato's Ladder', in particular, retains something of the play and the wit that I prize and would like to retain. But I think you're right that there is a movement – for several pressing and concurrent reasons – out of mere irony or out of the profane towards possibly (you might say) the transcendental.

Cambridge, 20 September 1989
(Broadcast: 3 December 1989)

Fleur Adcock

In 1984 Fleur Adcock published an essay about growing up during the war. This is how it ends:

> I learned to live with an almost permanent sense of free-floating, unfocused nostalgia, and with the combination of crushed humility and confident arrogance that comes from not quite belonging. It is no bad thing to be an outsider, if one wants to see places and events clearly enough to write about them. At any rate an outsider seemed to be what, after so much practice at it, I had become.

By 'practice' she means the experience of a childhood lived perpetually on the move, without the opportunity to put down roots. She was born in New Zealand in 1934; spent the whole of the Second World War in rural and suburban England, moving from lodging to lodging, school to school; then returned to Wellington at the age of thirteen, by now burdened with nostalgia for the many scenes of her childhood. She came back to Britain in 1963 and has lived here ever since.

In 1983 her highly praised *Selected Poems* appeared; it includes work from seven previous books. Her recent collections are *The Incident Book* (1986) and, subsequent to this interview, *Time Zones* (1991). Fleur Adcock is also a distinguished anthologist: she has edited *The Oxford Book of Contemporary New Zealand Verse* and *The Faber Book of Twentieth Century Women's Poetry*.

To what extent was your poetry formed in New Zealand? Were there New Zealand poets, for instance, whom you could think of as models when you were young?

Well, it depends how young. I married one when I was eighteen: Alastair Campbell. That must have been fairly significant. But I'd been writing since I was a child in England – I'd been writing since

I was six or seven. I didn't know there were such things as New Zealand poets – wouldn't have cared. When I went back, New Zealand poetry was getting off the ground. It was a fairly recent invention. It didn't really come into being until the Twenties and Thirties. I read the poets and I met them and knew them – James K. Baxter for example. I don't think I was influenced by them; I was too busy being influenced by what was more important to me, things that struck me with more dramatic force.

Which things, for instance?

In my teens it was Blake. I went all through the prophetic books, all those lovely sounds. Milton, Donne, Eliot. When I was about fifteen I discovered Eliot and went all disillusioned. Then later, when I went to University, I read Classics, and then there were some Latin poets: Catullus, Propertius – those were the people whose voices somehow got through to me. A highly personal style: the way they talked about their love affairs and their agonies and frustrations.

So initially quite a metaphysical or even transcendental bunch: Milton, Blake...

Maybe, yes. I hadn't seen that...

And you mention James K. Baxter, the New Zealand poet. I suppose in a sense he might be thought to fit in with that.

Yes, I think he probably does, although I don't really think of him as my kind of poet. But he was an enormous figure in New Zealand. Not physically – he was a small, hunched man with a deep lugubrious voice. He published his first collection when he was eighteen. He was a comet. He just startled everyone – enormous technical facility. He lived the life of a poet, he went through all sorts of agonies and transitions, he was an alcoholic, he was a Catholic convert, he ended up as a kind of Christian guru living in a community looking after young drug addicts, he was rebellious, he was out to shock everyone.

If he's not your kind of poet exactly, what kind of effect did he have on you?

I suppose we were a little bit short of hero figures in New Zealand and he seemed to be one. He was extremely famous, even when I was a student, and he was very encouraging to the young. Or the *younger*, I should say: I suppose he was eight years older than me, which seemed a lot at the time. He was a critic whose good opinion one was very glad to have, and he would read and encourage and discuss the work of young poets he liked.

You got his good opinion quite early on in fact.

Once I got started, yes, although I wasn't writing in a way that I
could call serious until I was in my mid-twenties, which was after I
was divorced from Alastair and starting my own life. I think I was
very overshadowed by the fact of being married to a poet.

Your first two books, The Eye of the Hurricane *and* Tigers, *both
have traces of what, very broadly speaking, we think of as the Fifties
manner – slightly Movementish.*

Yes, oh yes, I was into Larkin and all of those people.

*But under the surface of elegant scepticism, it seems to me, you're
already anticipating the kind of reversal that took place in the later
Sixties and early Seventies. Do you think that's a fair way of expressing it?*

I don't know, I haven't stood back from my own work sufficiently to
notice that it happened in that order, if it did. I'd thought that both
elements were going on simultaneously, all the time, that there were
irrational urges and surges. No, I wrote about dreams quite early on,
I think, if dreams are part of it. I'm always being accused of being
detached and classical and poised and cool and all of those words
which I suppose I would have found rather flattering when I was
younger. I thought I was just a heap of seething emotions and was
relieved to be taken for cool. But these adjectives stick because critics
look at the person who did the last crit; they often don't bother to
think up words of their own.

*You obviously feel a little irritated by those descriptions, yet you
must also feel that they have some point. Is it that you feel that,
when you're described as classical and cool and elegant, the kind of
irrational engine that drives the poem is not being sufficiently recognised?*

I'm not quite sure why I feel annoyed by it, except that it doesn't seem
to me to be true. But, of course, I do like things to be tidy: I have a
classical nature, I was a librarian for many years and I may also have
a cataloguer's mentality. I like grammar and punctuation and the
general elements of order in discourse. I quite like rhyme, I quite like
forms too. It's all a way of just putting a straitjacket around the mad,
wailing, hysterical self inside. I'm beginning to sound like Baxter!

*In some of your quite early poems there's a contrast that you make
between surface and depth. I think it runs right through the work,*

but it's specifically named in a couple of early poems, 'The Water Below' and 'Mornings After', where you talk about two kinds of dreams: the ones which have some sort of rational basis in pleasure or fear and those which confront things you'd really rather not confront.

Well, those are both based on dreams in a sense. 'The Water Below' was describing a misapprehension I had about houses when I was a small child: I imagined that there was water flowing underneath the house (although when you went under the house – as you could in New Zealand houses – there was no water there). So it's the subconscious, it's the great primal sea under everything. Then the other one is overtly about dreams, and especially the ones that you forget, that you wake up and can't believe – they're so revolting – the ones about eating worms and that sort of thing. Where are these impulses coming from?

Andrew Motion has said that you're very good 'at bed'. That is, at dream, illness and sex. Do you think of those things as being connected?

Well, they're connected in physical ways, in that they all relate to the body and to what happens to the unconscious mind: fever, hallucination and so on. I *am* interested in the decay of the body in illness, getting older, dying – and birth of course also, and sex, and dreams. Well, dreams are (as Graves says) the free show that we can have at night. I used to use dreams quite a lot when I was more insecure about my writing, I think, because I deliberately wanted some irrational input. But people's dreams are very boring to other people and now I would only use them if they had some definite connection with something in the outside world. I'm more interested in the outside world and other people than I used to be.

And so you get to a poem like 'The Soho Hospital For Women', for instance...

Yes, exactly – where it's the other people, the people in the next beds, who are of more interest to me in the end than my own experience. Being brought up against those extremes: danger, risk, despair, the experiences that were being had near me.

One of the things people don't very often say about your poems is that they are often very funny. I mean, when the critics are going on about the classical precision and grace, they don't actually say that some of them make you laugh.

Well, perhaps they didn't in the old days when I was being classically precise and graceful! I think humour is something that has become more important. I like making people laugh. It's easy to make them cry, anybody can make them cry – you just say a few poignant little things about death and they'll all be sobbing. But to make them laugh is a bit trickier. And *it's* an irrational thing too, humour. It has something in common with poetry, in that they both sometimes harness together two incongruous ideas. That's what makes a poem work. Trying to explain what a poem is is rather like trying to explain what a joke is. If people can't see it, then they can't see it – it's like what Louis Armstrong said about jazz: 'If you don't know, I can't tell you.'

There's another set of poems of yours which one of your blurb writers calls 'anti-erotic' poems. There's one rather famous example of this which is called 'Against Coupling'. They're anti-erotic in the sense that they're sexy but...

They're about how horrible men are!

Thank you so much! Does that mean they have a kind of feminist edge without being in any programmatic sense feminist poems?

I think I was a very late developer as a feminist. It took me a long time to realise that I wasn't just a man in some basic sense. The poets I modelled myself on were men and I earned my living and I got a mortgage and did all the things that men do. And then it leaked through somehow almost accidentally. Maybe 'Against Coupling' was one of the initial prods. It was written in the late Sixties, so it's been around for a long time. In fact, I wrote it just to bring one particular relationship to an end – it was really supposed to be a kick in the teeth for someone I was finished with. But it took on a universal application! It's only over the last ten years that I would have noticed that I was becoming a feminist or that I would have proclaimed that I am one. And that also happened rather slowly. Children, little girl children, female protagonists were getting into the poems – there's one called 'Blue Glass', there's one about Bethan and Bethany. Of course, you don't have much control. You don't sit down and say: 'I'm now going to write a poem about somebody who is this and represents that.' It just comes and you find you're writing it. Afterwards you get the rational explanations to give to the people who ask you things – the students who write to me and say: 'What does the Ex-Queen represent?' She doesn't represent anything – she represents what happens to a certain type of person who is brought up to please men, but at the time I was just seduced by the oddity of the phrase, 'The Ex-Queen Among the Astronomers'.

It seems to me that one of the things Sylvia Plath did was to invent or to borrow a whole set of new poetic personae that hadn't been around before, because most poems, after all, are written by men. So princesses and witches and people of that sort...

Yes, I'd been doing that. I was doing that princesses and witches bit in the late Fifties, early Sixties. But I think I got that out of Edwin Muir and his ilk, people who were writing about fairy tales and legends.

When you were a girl and you were reading Donne and Catullus and Milton and so on, were there any woman poets then that you were conscious of?

Very few. Almost none that I can remember. The first one who impinged, I suppose, was Edna St Vincent Millay when I was in my quite late teens. I would have been seventeen when I discovered her in *The Oxford Book of American Verse* and wandered along the beach quoting her to myself: all those ones about the death of love affairs. Great stuff when you're just embarking on one! I also liked the Bohemian lifestyle. I liked the idea that she led a rather liberated life, which anybody growing up in the Fifties in New Zealand would have found rather hard to do, or to get away with.

Has she stayed with you? I mean, she's an obvious stimulus to an adolescent imagination, but does she mature with age like a good wine?

There are some new ones I discovered when I was doing the reading for my Faber anthology, but I continue to admire her craftsmanship. That's something I always do admire in poets anyway: if they can make things work in the mechanical way, if things are well put together.

One of the things about Edna St Vincent Millay that I find a little odd is that, you know, if you've written a rather sentimental love poem, somebody will say: 'Oh that's almost as bad as Edna St Vincent Millay, isn't it?' I don't actually feel this.

No, I think that's a confusion; I think they've got some sort of multiple American poet, an all-purpose female with three names – they may be thinking of Ella Wheeler Wilcox or various other people and they've decided to put this label on to this not quite actual person.

You mentioned your anthology, which is The Faber Book of Twentieth Century Women's Poetry. *Edna St Vincent Millay figures quite prominently near the beginning of that book, doesn't she? Do you see her as one of the 'foremothers', or whatever we call the ancestors of woman achievers?*

No doubt she is, yes – although what I wanted to reveal was what British women were doing. I just wanted to show that women were still writing and always had been, that throughout this century they had been writing in interesting and varied ways and had sunk into oblivion in the backs of secondhand-book shops and the shelves of poetry libraries.

Having to work your way through all that material and make selections from it: did that in some way feed back into your own poetry?

Probably not initially, no. I don't know whether it did or not, but always the immediate effect of reading a lot of other people's poetry is that you don't write your own, particularly when it's a question of selecting, not just reading someone for pleasure. Judging a competition or, I suppose, editing a magazine or any activity where you read a lot of other people's poetry just numbs the thing in you that might be tempted to add to this large mass of print.

Do you think women are going to need to go on fighting for separate recognition in this way, or do you think we've yet begun to reach a point where we can forget about these distinctions between male and female poets?

I think we should be more or less there by now. We're certainly getting there. It was a phase. I hope it was just a phase anyway; I wouldn't like to think that things were still going to be segregated. But I do get annoyed when I go into bookshops and see a section called 'Women's Interests', and you go over there and that's where you find Stevie Smith or Marianne Moore, as though the sex was more important than the poetry. But it needed to be said and proved. I hope it's clear now that women can do it.

Do you now feel more confident about your own position in the poetry world?

Well, I didn't really feel that my gender was a disadvantage, I didn't feel that it was something I had to struggle against. I think being a

New Zealander was more of a disadvantage: growing up in the wrong place from the point of view of British editors, and being rather late at getting going because of things like family. So I didn't see being female very much as a disadvantage. Maybe I was just lucky. I arrived at a time when poetry readings were beginning. People quite liked to have a female on the bill and there weren't many of us around unfortunately. Now, well, we're everywhere.

London, 26 September 1989
(Broadcast: 2 February 1990)

James Fenton

James Fenton has spent much of his life working as a foreign correspondent. He has reported from Vietnam and Cambodia, from the two Germanies (as they then were), and from the Philippines. He has written about war and its aftermath. His poetry is haunted by what he calls 'the memory of war'. The role of traveller and observer seems to have contributed to his poetic persona; even when war is not the subject, he is essentially the compassionate outsider.

What it does not account for is his versatility: he also writes nonsense verse (in the tradition of Edward Lear and Lewis Carroll) and, in more modernist vein, 'found' poems. The independence of Fenton's taste has recently led him into conflict with the current guardians of poetic convention – literary academics in American universities.

He is not a prolific poet. He was only 22 when he published his first book, but eleven years had to elapse before the major collection that was to make his name: *The Memory of War and Children in Exile* (1983). Then another ten years went by before his latest book, *Out of Danger*. At the time of this interview, *Out of Danger* had not yet appeared, though an important interim publication had. This was *The Manila Envelope* (1989), which contained – as well as some boldly lyrical poems – a polemical manifesto. The latter, a characteristic blend of playfulness and pugnacity, announces the new style he christens 'the New Recklessness'.

You were very young when you began publishing. How did you start writing?

I suppose I started when I was a schoolboy. I started by writing quite a lot of parodies of the kind of things that other people were doing, or poems in protest against what was considered OK poetry at the time. You remember there was a very strong feeling that poetry ought to be free verse – haikus were healthy and so on and so forth. Some friends and I at school wrote completely against all that. Then, when I went to Oxford, I went in for a poetry prize they have there. They used to set extremely recondite subjects. That pleased me very much, because my subject in my first year at Oxford was set by Edmund Blunden and it was 'The Opening of Japan, 1853-4'. I decided I'd write a sonnet-sequence about that and then went and read it up. That was how it began.

Interestingly you started with poetry as essentially a craft and also something which is capable of light entertainment and perhaps a little subversion.

I don't think I thought of it as a craft really. It was more like an act of rebellion.

You were also rebellious in other ways, weren't you? I mean, you were pretty political – perhaps still are.

That came later on. I was pretty fundamentally unpolitical at that stage – although things began to change in '68, when I saw Czechoslovakia during the Prague Spring. In fact I left the day before the tanks went in.

So when did you become a Marxist exactly? I mean you had a period in the International Socialists, didn't you?

Yes, that was in '69 – a bit after everybody else. I didn't have a political 1968. I missed out on most of that.

Nevertheless, there is a faintly 1968 atmosphere in one or two of the poems in your first book and then shortly after that you went to Vietnam and Cambodia, didn't you?

Yes, that was quite a time after that. That was in '73. By then, I'd already spent some time working in London as Assistant to the Literary Editor on the *New Statesman*. I started in literary journalism, but what I really wanted to do was to become a reporter, so I moved gradually to political journalism. Then, after my first book had come out, I went off to Vietnam.

You've written a well-known series of poems about Cambodia: 'Dead Soldiers', 'In a Notebook', 'Cambodia' and then, later, 'Children in Exile'. When did you write those?

Much, much later. The one called 'Dead Soldiers' was written *years* later – after I'd finally decided that I couldn't fulfil a contract for writing a book about Cambodia. So I paid off my advance and the day afterwards I thought, 'Well, I've got this thing that was going to go in that book,' and I just sat down and wrote it. But all those poems came a long time after. I found that I couldn't write about Cambodia for a long time afterwards – not while the Khmer Rouge were in power and very little news was coming out apart from grim news. I just couldn't. After the Khmer Rouge fell I found that some of my friends had survived. I went to the refugee camps and then met up with some people and after that I could write a bit about it. But by that time the opportunity for writing in detail about it had gone.

It's often seemed to me that you make use of writing that is already available. This is most obviously the case in those early 'found' poems you wrote. But you also make use of your reading and previous bits of your own writing. It's as if you raid it periodically.

That's true. The incident in 'Dead Soldiers': I think I described that in an article in the *New Statesman* years before writing the poem. I studied psychology and, at Oxford, that means experimental psychology; it involves reading a lot of scientific papers for instance. I found a great sort of poetry in these scientific papers. I wasn't really understanding what I was reading, but I was enjoying it for purely aesthetic reasons.

So in a sense you're finding a kind of poetry in the authenticity of the language, as opposed to something which is previously assumed to be poetic?

Yes. The interest in those days was finding the poetic in almost strictly non-poetic surroundings, non-poetic materials.

The other thing about those Cambodian poems is that the strength of them derives from what might be thought their weakness, which is that you're an outsider. I suppose if you had written them while you were actually there observing what was going on, they might have a voyeuristic quality. But, looking back on the experience, they take on a certain quality of pathos: something that can't be got out of the mind.

I certainly had a horror of the idea of going there and then writing more poems. It would be a terrible pose to adopt. When I was in those countries, I was there as a journalist. That was the work I was doing there.

*This characteristic that I've just described of being an observer look-
ing back with pathos also seems to come into some of the less overtly
political poems. There's a group of poems which contain narrative
material: 'Nest of Vampires', 'A Vacant Possession', one or two
others. In each of those poems there's a narrator, who is somehow
removed from the action...*

There are different narrators in those poems. I had this idea at the
time that I would do a series of poems called 'Landscapes and
Rooms', so what I was thinking of wasn't actually the narrative so
much as having a certain landscape, certain interiors of different
kinds. The first one of the poems turned out to be 55 lines long and
they were all going to be 55 lines long – an insane way of working
– I don't recommend it to anybody else. But that was the idea. The
personae are very different: one is a child in the nineteenth century,
whose father's fortune seems to have gone up in smoke, and another
is a Risorgimento revolutionary. That poem was written after a holiday on the island of Panarea, just north of Sicily, which was a prison
island.

*A number of your poems have a faintly riddling quality to them. Is
that a deliberate device?*

No, I think perhaps less so now; that was then. The poem called 'A
Vacant Possession' was another 'what-I-did-in-my-holidays' poem.
Some friends and I went to this part of France and we saw this house
and walked around it and we all had the fantasy of what would you
do living in such a house. I developed the fantasy in the poem just for
as long as the fantasy would last. It can't last beyond a certain point
– it fades away.

Could you say that the end of the poem is your exit from the fantasy?

The end of the poem goes something like: 'The curtains move. The
light sways. The cold sets in.' That's purely autobiographical. I was
living in the East End of London at the time. The house was pretty
derelict and I came home one day at the time I was finishing this
poem to find that somebody, assuming it to be completely derelict,
had smashed all the windows in it. So I was sitting there in this room
with broken windows finishing the poem and I just bunged that into it.

*The other cryptic kind of poem that you write is nonsense poetry or
a kind of wildly humorous verse – poems like 'The Kingfisher's Box-
ing Gloves' and 'The Killer Snails'. Do you think of these as jeux
d'esprit or are they an integral part of the main endeavour?*

Well, what is a *jeu d'esprit*? There is an element of the game in poetry, there is certainly an element of the spirit in poetry. So if I had to choose between the two options you give me, I suppose I'd have to say that it's an integral part of the endeavour. That doesn't stop it being a *jeu d'esprit* as well. I've always liked nonsense poetry. Perhaps the affection that you have for it derives from the fact that you tend to be introduced to it as a child and it remains with you as the kind of poetry that you read as a child and which you always enjoyed and found fun.

There's a recent poem of yours called 'The Ballad of the Shrieking Man', which is a sort of nonsense poem. It seems to combine your preoccupation with nonsense and the concern with political situations and public horrors. Is that something that you were aware of in writing it?

You know, when you see these guys walking down the street shrieking at the tops of their voices, you can't help sympathising with them. I used to see them in the East End of London walking down Mile End Road and places like that, and really they seem to be making a pretty straightforward comment on their surroundings. The surroundings in this poem are more exotic – they have a kind of Eastern European flavour I suppose. But these are the guys who suddenly perceive what's happening and are driven mad by it. Yes.

How did you write that poem?

I had the idea for the rhythm of what they would shriek and, once I had got that and worked out one stanza of it, I was able to write the rest. I had a very strong idea of a musical metre and I had a strong feeling that it should have dance with it. There are lots of counter-rhythms that you don't hear but I hear and there should be playing of spoons and all kinds of things like that going on with it. The story really came to me in a dream and, once the principle of the story was there, that bit was easy to get through – just telling that tale. It's probably one of the first poems in English to have been written on a prawn pond: I wrote it in the Philippines surrounded by prawn workers who were slightly surprised to hear me reading it out.

And beating the spoons presumably?

Yes, and jumping around.

You're writing a number of kinds of poem – nonsense poems are just one kind – that nobody else seems to be attempting at the moment, yet I recently saw you described in a TLS *controversy as an 'Establishment poet'. Did you recognise yourself in that phrase?*

'An Establishment poet'. I suppose there might be some justice in it, though actually I think I've always taken a rather adversarial view aesthetically. When I was an undergraduate, for instance, it was very unfashionable to like Auden. I admired Auden tremendously and always felt he was being very unjustly dealt with by critics and poets at the time. That animus against Auden has gone now, has been forgotten, but that was the kind of context I began writing in. The context in which I write at the moment is, I think, out of adversarial feeling towards several trends in the current aesthetic, particularly in America. I spent some time, recently, teaching in America and found an absolute terror of doing the straightforward poetic thing. So if I now write a very plain lyric, it's actually in protest against people writing in a very muzzy, neither-here-nor-there, anti-metrical, very cautious, take-it-or-leave-it style, that seems to have been forced on them by the Academy.

So there's a paradox here: people like Marjorie Perloff, who attacked you, or Helen Vendler, whom you've attacked, are championing a kind of avant-garde *poetry, but it's an* avant-garde *that has become very safe and is protected by an academic Establishment...*

...and has no audience. It's very interesting that poets in America have very little by way of a readership or audience in general. They depend on the Academy very strongly. In England what's happened is that poetry has built up more and more of an audience and so you can talk about having a readership. Poetry here is much much more popular than it is in the States.

Does this tendency in America make you anxious about the future of poetry?

Not the future of poetry in England, as I said, because I think that we are quite different. We've always retained our connection with the past, with tradition, and we've managed to re-establish rapport with many readers.

In 'The Manila Manifesto' you seem to be suggesting that you want poetry to become a much more expansive, entertaining kind of art.

Yes, entertaining, if that's the appropriate word for the particular poem. Yes, the spirit that I would like to see is much more poetry that makes bold gestures, that paints in bright colours, that has strong up-front rhythms, that has honest-to-goodness rhymes instead of whingey half-rhymes. I mean, half-rhymes are very nice and so on, but bold rhymes – that's what's the thing of the future, the fashionable thing!

And are the prospects good?

We shall see. It will take a bit of time. When people start saying it's out of fashion, then we'll know we've succeeded.

London, 31 January 1990
(Broadcast: 3 March 1990)

György Petri

György Petri, who was born in 1943, is regarded by many of his fellow-Hungarians as the most original poet of his generation. Some would also say he is the best: high praise in a country which, this century alone, has produced several major poets – Attila József, Miklós Radnóti and Sándor Weöres among them. Though Petri speaks respectfully of his forebears, he has decisively parted company with them where poetic method is concerned. Hungarian Modernism is rooted in Romanticism. Petri has discarded its rhetoric in favour of a language that is harsh, spare and ironic. He eschews overt attempts at idealism, pathos or beauty; what grips us in his poetry is its force and uncompromising truthfulness. As he says in a recent poem on the execution of Imre Nagy (who led the reformist government of 1956): 'My eyes are dry. I need them for looking with.'

For many years, Petri stood out against the government's control of publishing, his books appearing only in *samizdat*. Since the weakening of the Communist regime early in 1989, however, five books have been legally published with some commercial success. A selection of his work has now appeared in English: *Night Song of the Personal Shadow*, translated by George Gömöri and myself. In March 1990, as Hungary went to the polls for her first free elections since the end of the Second World War, I interviewed Petri in a Budapest café.

Are you involved in the election at all?

Only as an elector, not as a potential elected. It's a very interesting thing that, for me, these so-called democratic changes mean that I am not obliged to participate in political life any more. There will be a new age, the aged of professional politicians, and I'm not obliged at every moment of my life to be a *citoyen*. I mean to be a *bourgeois*!

You mean that, as things were under Communism, you had to be political all the time?

I had to because it was a moral obligation, because there was no normal canalisation for the expression of political opinion. Now I hope that the parties will solve this problem and that normal parliamentary life can fulfil all these tasks, and I hope that I will have the opportunity to be a dissident in another meaning of the word.

Is it going to be difficult for you as a poet now, in the sense that the business of writing poetry has been so much involved with opposition and anger and contempt?

Just what I would say is that in a totalitarian system political life is over-dramatised. One can say that political life is very poetic. In a normal democracy the political life is very prosaic…and boring. I hope that we are now beginning to live with a boring political life! I never feel (as a poet concerned with political life) an obligation or *engagement*. For me politics, the political life, was a theme, a *motif*, and I was engaged in political activities as a man, but not as a poet. I was concerned in a lot of my poetry with politics, but because it was interesting, because it was dramatic…but now everything's changed.

There's a poem of yours I like very much, which is called 'Electra'. It always seems to me that what that says, partly, is that the poet has to be somehow negative, to be destructive.

Yes, I am quite sure that the main function of poetry – if poetry *has* a function – is a destructive one. But at the same time I think that is a positive function. 'Electra' is one of the most important poems I've written. But it says quite precisely that Electra isn't concerned with the day-to-day problems of political or social life, but the main moral tensions…

When did you start writing poetry?

In the very early period of the Kádár system.* I published my first poem in '61. In '61 I was seventeen years old.

Very young.

Very young, and after this first publication there were other publications, but when I was twenty years old I stopped writing poems

---

* János Kádár, General Secretary of the Hungarian Socialist Workers Party, 1956 – 1989.

because I thought what I was writing was very conventional and boring. There was a long pause in my poetry: I stopped at twenty and began again when I was 26.

What enabled you to start again?

It was that I met with the poetry of Eliot. Eliot's poems appeared in Hungarian translation – in the translation of István Vas – and this volume had a decisive and liberating influence on me. Perhaps because – this is my own interpretation – T.S. Eliot showed the possibility of combining everyday life and everyday language with deeper philosophical and cultural problems, and the possibility of realising poetry without pathos or rhetoric.

I was talking earlier about being destructive. One wouldn't exactly say that Eliot was destructive but Eliot is not life-enhancing. He is negative and pessimistic and ironic...

Irony is the other very important *motif* for me, because the main themes of Hungarian – not only Hungarian but East European – poetry are lacking in irony. It was a very simple and in this sense liberating influence that I had the experience that one can write poems in this way. Because formerly I could not imagine that it was possible.

So, I suppose that in the Hungarian tradition there was the necessary political awareness but it was a political awareness combined with rhetoric. Is that it?

Mm. I think that, in the whole of Eastern Europe, political problems are unavoidable, because politics has so strongly ruled everyday life there that in an artistic sense it has been unavoidable; there are practically no important poets or novelists in Eastern Europe who have been able to avoid the political sphere. But I have to repeat that that is in the artistic sense; it means no *engagement* in the Bolshevik sense. There is the simple problem of every artist who wants in some sense to give a description of the conditions in which we are living. I disliked the Marxist concept of realism...

Can you say why?

Because the concept of realism has a normative and hierarchical content, and in this sense I reject realism as a norm. It can be a programme or possibility for me but I can imagine quite other possibilities, quite other ways.

Did Eliot's politics help you in any way to oppose such concepts?

You are saying that Eliot had his own political views, very conservative ones, but I was not influenced by them. I am not a conservative, I am not a Christian, but for me it was important that he pointed to the possibility that one can write in the same poem about one's ideological crisis and the crisis of culture and about the very simple facts of life: the connection of these two spheres was important for me, not so much the philosophy of Eliot, which is quite apart.

No, I was just thinking simply that people in the West tend to think of conservatives as people who support the existing system, but of course Eliot is not a conservative of that sort; he's in opposition.

Yes...I have to make a distinction between the political or philosophical content of a poet's poetry and other views. The poems themselves, Eliot's poems, are very destructive and absolutely not conservative.

Can you tell me how you became an opposition poet? I mean, your first two books were officially accepted, weren't they? How did it happen that you stopped being accepted?

I became a poet of opposition because the totalitarian state made me one. It was not my aim, not my programme. Very simply, I wrote my poems, but I am very devoted to myself and I wanted to write my own poems, and there was official rejection. Perhaps it's interesting that I was always ideologically suspect for the regime...and it began before I wrote my first directly political things. The smell.

But there must have come a moment when you became intolerable to the regime. I mean, up to a point they had tolerated you and then, around the time you began publishing in samizdat...

The actual cause was that originally my first *samizdat* book, *Eternal Monday*, was offered to an official publishing house, but they told me I had to throw out more than thirty poems from this book, and then I said it was impossible because, without these poems, the volume would suffer a change. So they offered me a compromise that left out a lot of poems, and I said no...It's another story why later it happened, in '81, that one of my friends created an illegal *samizdat* publishing house which worked very effectively: more than fifty publications.

So your book was rejected by the publisher in 1980. By that time, were you already involved in the unofficial opposition in the country?

Yes. I was the editor of perhaps the most important *samizdat* opposition periodical, *Beszélő*, and I was a founder of a fund for support of the poor, and I took part in the pro-Solidarity demonstrations. I put my signature to Charter 77. In 1980 we organised a children's camp at Lake Balaton for Polish children – and I was a cook!

So the political situation for you got much more serious in Hungary in the late 1970s, early 1980s. Is that right?

A little more complicated: I think the crisis began after 1968 in Prague. Since 1968, I have thought socialism unreformable. But you are right that economic and political decay began about '73 or '74. I think that '74 was a beginning: one could feel from day to day that something was going wrong; and from those years I became more and more sure that their policies must be changed.

During the time of your samizdat *publication, were you persecuted very much?*

In comparison with my Czechoslovak or Romanian or Soviet or East German colleagues, not so much. What actually happened was a complete prohibition of publishing, but I was not banished, was not arrested. It belongs to the essence of the Kádár regime that it *was* a dictatorship, but in a milder form. When I compare my situation with that of Milan Kundera – he was exiled. And Václav Havel was a prisoner. In Hungary there was a more sophisticated dictatorship – one can say a more clever dictatorship than in Czechoslovakia. In Czechoslovakia and in East Germany there was a more stupid form of dictatorship.

Do you think that the milder dictatorship exerts a stronger level of control over people?

Not a stronger but a deeper: a greater corruption of the moral state of the people. So I think that our dictatorship was no more sympathetic than the stronger ones. Perhaps more dangerous.

So that's what your poems are, isn't it – a refusal to be corrupted?

Yes, this is what is essential for me. The relevance of politics for me was to defend my personal integrity. And therefore, because now we are beginning to live under conditions of normal social life, it has no very great importance any more.

I wonder if you can tell me a bit about the way you use language in poems? I mean, one of the things that's very striking to me about

your poems – though it sounds a little silly to say so – is that they're
very moral poems, very pure, but the language of them is very
impure. It's full of obscenity and slang and word-play, and it's a very
mixed kind of language. Are you conscious of how you began to
write like that?

My use of language was partly a provocation against the unbelievable prudery of socialist realism and state culture. This prudery
means two things. First, it is a rejection of sexual life and bodily func-
tions. There's a great silence about this area of life. And the other
sense is a sociological prudery, a refusal to speak about the disturbing facts of social or private life. A canonised language of state
culture developed and just what I want to destroy is this language.
Poetry lives only in the language and to create a new poetry you have
to create a new language.

The Romantic rhetoric of earlier Hungarian poetry – of the nine-
teenth-century or early twentieth-century poets – do you feel that
that's been corrupted – retrospectively – by state socialism?

You must make a distinction between the tradition itself and the
canonised, obligatory tradition. I very much like a lot of Hungarian
Romantic poets, but not as a canon for me.

No, I'm sure: I didn't mean you didn't like them, but in some way
that that sort of idealism has been claimed by the Communist
Party...

No, I think what really happened was that the Communist Parties in
Eastern Europe felt that they seemed for most of the population
foreign. A system forced upon them by the USSR. And therefore they
tried to show themselves as very traditionalist and nationalist and
full of patriotism and convention. But the Soviet system itself, if you
see the average cultural production of Stalinism, that was a narrow
classicism or neo-Baroque. So-called revolutionary art was pro-
hibited in the Stalin period. And then they emphasised traditionalist
standards – good old morals and so on. I think these regimes felt that
the only possibility was to make themselves acceptable to the people
by traditionalism. But at the same time, of course, it means not the
whole tradition but only a very selected one – *ad usum Delphini*. For
example, Swift's *Gulliver* for children, so that it was a tradition for
children. What was selected was at the same time canonised. So it
means that, when I went to *Gymnasium*, I learned from Hungarian
schoolbooks that Milton is very progressive because he supported

Cromwell. Shakespeare of course, very good, but not always progressive. Keats: yeah, very good poet, but a bourgeois decadent. Burns: very progressive too, but...

Did they know about Burns's obscene poems?

But these obscene poems we could not read!

Do you support a particular party now?

I am a member of the Alliance of Free Democrats but only a simple member. I write political articles for their paper sometimes, and I participate in demonstrations and meetings, but I wouldn't like a professional political role.

Do you have any fears about these changes in your country?

I have fears because I think that these very positive political changes have developed under very bad economic conditions, and perhaps you have heard about the tragic events in Transylvania. There is the possibility that, under these bad economic conditions, a part of the population will feel dissatisfied – dissatisfied and intolerant, because we are free but...no food. For example, this fighting in Romania. I fear the nationalists among the East European peoples and the unbelievable development of particularism and regionalism inside each country. For example, in Czechoslovakia: Slovak separatism against the Czechs, Moravian separatists too, the separatist movement of Czechoslovak Germans, and the Hungarian minority. So I have to say that it's very good that socialism is over, because socialism was a catastrophe, but the outlook is very very uncertain.

Budapest, 23 March 1990

Donald Davie

Donald Davie's life has been ruled by poetry. Now retired, he has spent the whole of his adult life not just writing poetry but teaching it too, as critic, scholar, editor and professor. He has been awesomely prolific: at a rough count, there are sixteen books of criticism and fourteen books of poetry, including two volumes of *Collected Poems*. And those figures take no account of his work as editor, translator, book-reviewer and essayist.

Davie's strength as a writer derives from internal conflict. At the start of his career, for instance, he was associated with that reaction against Modernism known as the Movement. As he developed, though, an early fascination with the achievement of Ezra Pound grew with him and worked against the grain of his natural conservatism. He has never quite lost the disciplined formality of his first book, *Brides of Reason*, but the textures of his verse have roughened considerably.

His most recent book, *To Scorch or Freeze*, is technically his most radical. The book is a sequence of fractured, free-verse psalms, which embody – rather than describe – the problems of a sacred language in a pluralist age. Davie's recent work disarmingly reveals a temperament – candid, irascible and vulnerable – which the orderly quatrains of his early books held in check.

To anyone unfamiliar with your work those two books, To Scorch or Freeze *and* Brides of Reason, *might seem to have been written by two different people. How do you account for that?*

Well, I'm a restless person, rightly or wrongly; I don't like doing again what I've done once. Of course, over and above that, there's the pressure of experience. I mean, outside of poetry and writing, you have experiences which turn you into a significantly different person, and plainly the styles that you work out when you're a young man...

well they *shouldn't* be still serving you when you're middle-aged. It would seem to me that, if they were, it would mean that you'd been at a standstill in your psychological development. Indeed, to be irascible – as you want me to be – I would say that those of my contemporaries who rather notably have *not* changed from first to last are the ones who need to explain themselves.

Can we perhaps focus on a particular aspect of the development? I'm thinking about metre and form and so on. The new book is in a broken kind of free verse, and the early book – you called yourself at that time 'A pasticheur of late-Augustan styles' – is very smooth. How did that development take place? Was it gradual or did you go through a sudden change in attitude?

No, it was gradual and, at the risk of seeming very mechanical or mechanistic about it, I can be quite plain. Those smooth pentameters that I wrote for my first collection, usually arranged in rhyming quatrains, I got too much in command of them and they came too easy: the style was writing me, the style was using me – or so I felt – so I wanted to change then and there. The first change was to shorten the measure and, if you really look, if you think it's worthwhile, you will see (over fifteen or twenty years) me gradually shortening from a pentameter – a ten syllable line – to a tetrameter and a trimeter, by and large. In fact, *To Scorch or Freeze* – I think you're right to say that the style here is fractured; I'm not sure that you're right to say that it's free verse. Some of it is, but a lot of it is still basically in trimeters, six syllable lines. I find it hard to write genuine free verse and really what looks like verse that is hard to scan, which I've written, I think if you look at it you'll find that it's scannable but in a very rough and ready fashion. This is by way of being a sort of sadness for me. I would like to have been able to handle free or unmetred verse more often than I do.

You mean in the manner of Pound, for instance: that kind of free verse?

That kind of cadence and rhythm, yes, abundantly. I hope I would not have to pay the price for it that Pound had to pay in terms of breaking up sentences and abandoning grammar, but yes, of course, I do think that Pound was in his generation the most inventive ear of any of the modern poets in our language.

Bringing in the name of Ezra Pound is to name somebody who has played a hugely important part in your career, and I think it would be true to say – without any dispraise to you – that when one looks back over your work one is struck by the presence of certain key influences. Does that make you derivative in some way?

It's very strange actually. It begins with the sheerest accident. When I was still a schoolboy in south Yorkshire and just going to be put up for an open scholarship at either Oxford or Cambridge, we had a change of headmaster. The new man who came was younger than the old head. He wasn't in fact a literary fellow at all, but he was very ambitious for the school that he'd moved to and he wanted to pot-hunt us, and so he said: 'Well, I think you'd better read some Ezra Pound. Not many of them will be reading Ezra Pound and, if you can let the examiners know that, it should stand you in good stead.' So, lo and behold, there I was in the sixth form of Barnsley Grammar School, in 1939 I suppose, reading in a baffled way 'Hugh Selwyn Mauberley' by Ezra Pound. And, of course, Pound is a particularly difficult master to have to confess to because, quite apart from his alarming and worse than alarming political and racist views, I am very well aware that some people are just rubbed up the wrong way by the whole of Pound's temperament and character – particularly as it shows up in his correspondence. And indeed I have moments – or rather more than moments, I have *phases* – in which I am exasperated by the old boy. Well, then I oscillate and I swing back... And I'll say one more thing: Pound is obviously a much less perfect poet than others, like T.S. Eliot or W.B. Yeats or Wallace Stevens or Thomas Hardy – we could go on. But it's precisely because he is imperfect that his juniors, I think, can learn from him. It's like a marble quarry where blocks of marble have been hewn away from the cliff but they've never yet been carried away to the studio to be actually finished or shaped by Michelangelo.

How does Pound influence people? How does he affect them?

Well in my case I think particularly through his insistence, in season and out of season, that you cannot write poetry that matters in English if you are taking account only of poetry *in* English. In other words, the importance of foreign bodies of poetry. It so happens that I am not a good linguist, or at any rate I'm a very lazy one, so that I am dependent much of the time on translations, and if I can't find translations that I trust, then I must sit down and slog at them myself, which is what I did with Boris Pasternak for instance. But that's one thing that I think Pound tells you, shows you. Another thing is that he was always quite plain that poetry was only one of the arts, that there's something wrong with a poet if he cannot respond to sculpture or architecture. The arts are all one. And I found that immensely rewarding in all sorts of ways.

You mention translation and poetry from foreign languages and it's obvious that that has had a huge importance for you – particularly, I suppose, poetry from the Slavic countries. How does poetry in a foreign language find its way into an English poet's work?

Well, in the case of this English poet, he, in about 1960, got very bored with what it was he had been doing. He wasn't going to disown it, but I didn't want to do any more of it. I discovered that I needed a model to show me what could be done and the model that I found was Boris Pasternak. I'm not sure why, but I think that his being in a foreign language – and a foreign language that I do not know, except very imperfectly, myself – enabled me, allowed me to find a voice, which was still my voice and yet a different voice from the one I'd been using. And I can't conceive that a poet in the English language could have done that for me. I may be wrong. But then of course I think you have to say there are perceptions in certain foreign languages such as we just do not have in English. That is to say, we have a wonderfully rich language of course, but it is not exhaustive of human experience – not by any means – and so we take pride in our language rightly and draw upon its riches, but every time we go to a first rate foreign poet in fact we're discovering that our language, rich and flexible as it is, can still be put under strain and extended; and indeed our experience – not just our linguistic experience – our experience can be extended. And that's what a foreign poet does.

Is it something to do with Pasternak's imagery that you learnt from particularly?

No, I would have said not, except in a very extended sense. His images are most often from the world of outdoors, from as we say nature, and of course it's Russian outside nature too. And I am not a person to whom the natural world matters – perhaps not as much as it should. I mean, I'm glad it's there and I notice when it's beautiful and when it isn't, but…I'm no gardener, for instance, I'm no longer any great walker over the hills and through the woods. Pasternak, like some other people in my life, continually alerted me, washed my senses clean, so that I could respond to those aspects of experience as keenly as I did naturally to other sorts. And that is the release that I was aware of when I began writing poems on his model.

The other thing that strikes a reader of those early poems, which you

seem to have had a running battle with throughout your career, is a
habit of irony. Can you comment on that at all?

Yes, yes. There are, aren't there, at least two sorts of irony, at least
two – many people have said this. It often seems that the world, the
cosmos, is treating us ironically. When Thomas Hardy spoke of
ironies of circumstance, he meant that: the way that, without our
intending it, life itself and our life-history trap us into our absurd
contradictions. That's *one* sort of irony – I suppose it includes tragic
irony. The other sort of irony is the sort that goes along with being
ironical, and that isn't what the universe does to us, but the stance
that we can adopt towards the universe – to get by, to be ironical
about it, so as to keep our composure. Well, I think a lot of young
poets very greatly value that second sort of irony. I know I did and
there's a great deal of irony of that sort in my earliest collections. But
it is ultimately defensive and protective, that sort of irony. As you
grow older, if you learn any sort of courage at all, you see that it is
defensive and you'll want to come out from behind that camouflage.
But as you rightly say, it has never been easy for me to do so. I don't
like to think of myself as in any way a confessional poet, for instance,
who plainly does without irony. In other words, I like to keep my
self-respect before my reader, to maintain my own privacies, and
irony is always one way of doing that. But, of course, particularly
with this last work, it's no good trying to be ironical with or about
the Psalms of David, and that's what I very much discovered.

Something that strikes me as we're talking is that, at key moments in
your career, you seem to have made decisions to extend your sensi-
bility by an act of will. Is that how you work?

Ye-es. Except that of course there are extensions that you cannot
make. I mean the sensibility just is not available to be wilfully mani-
pulated. I give an example which isn't much to my advantage: there
is no hope of my ever extending by an act of will my very limited
appreciation of music – whether classical music or popular music or
whatever. This is one of the arts which . . . I can take it or leave it. And
this of course cuts me off from a lot of people, including several who
are very close to me. I've tried in a baffled sort of way to listen to
records and see why they've mattered so much to my wife, but there's
a block there and I can't go beyond it, I can't get through there.

I was thinking in particular of a poem that you wrote years ago called
'With the Grain', where you seem to be – I say 'seem to be' because
it's rather obscure in places – where you seem to be talking about this
problem of working against your own temperament.

Yes, I think I am – in that poem and in others. What I've just said of course is that you can only do this up to a point; the grain tells after a while. It's related, you know, to a poet whom I don't often invoke – not nowadays – W.B. Yeats, talking about how the self calls up its anti-self, and some of that goes on. And that image of 'against the grain' – I agree with you that I got it rather obscure in places – but it seems to me wonderfully rich. I mean, if you're a sculptor from the stone, there's a grain in the stone which you have to respect – you can't force the chisel any way you want. Still more of course if you're a woodcarver. So that the resistance of the material to the will of the artist who is trying to shape it, there's an element of going against the grain in that quite literally. There's a grain in the stone and a grain in the wood and you can go against it up to a point, but only up to a point.

When you talk about the resistance of the material there with regard to poetry, what exactly does 'material' stand for in that metaphor?

Oh yes, that's very interesting. The material is language, obviously. The medium, the material, for us as writers is the words of our language in the structures that they take on. That is what confronts us as certainly as the marble or the granite confronts the sculptor. This, I think, is difficult for some people to conceive, though I do not believe it is difficult for the good poet in the act of composing. And that is where, you see, there is a resistance built into the whole operation. You are pushing against the language, which has its own grain, which has its own tendencies, and only up to a certain point can you afford to buck the laws inherent in the material. This is why I have no sympathy, and really never have had sympathy, with the rather many people who think that the conventions of – for instance – grammar in the English sentence are things which your true, impatient poet must break through. Or the people who are sure that they have a poet when they discover that he is not punctuating. This, it seems to me, most often produces the sort of poetry which I least admire and least like. It derives from the notion that language, our medium, is as infinitely malleable as plasticine – you can push it whatever way you like and mix the colours. I don't believe that's true, and I think that for an artist to think that is almost fatal, because it means that the necessary tension between himself and the material he's confronting has disappeared.

London, 19 March 1990
(Broadcast: 8 May 1990)

Patricia Beer

Patricia Beer once wrote a poem about a concert in a country church. When the interval comes, the audience pours out into the sunshine and open air:

> They spread all over the churchyard. They scan
> The crowd, recognize, smile and shake hands.
> By each tombstone a well-dressed person stands.
> It looks just like the Resurrection.

I am reminded of Stanley Spencer and the Resurrection in Cookham churchyard. Like Spencer, Patricia Beer depicts a familiar, everyday world that often seems on the point of settling, unaware, into attitudes of transcendence. An ironic tone of voice, however, is usually there to hold this possibility at bay.

It is significant, I think, that Patricia Beer, who was born into a Plymouth Brethren family, never quite surrenders the everyday to the otherworldly, in spite of an evident temptation to do so. She was born in Devon in 1919 and, although she's spent several years in London and Italy, she has felt the pull of the South-West for most of her life. She has published nine books of verse, including a severely pruned *Collected Poems*. She has also published a novel, an autobiography and some critical writings, which include a study of the Metaphysical poets, those masters of the ordinary and transcendent.

Her new book, *Friend of Heraclitus*, was published in 1993.

Another religious poet, John Milton, figures in a poem you wrote about your father, and I wonder, did poetry figure prominently in your childhood?

Yes, it was very important indeed. Mostly because of school. My father's feeling about Milton was that Milton was a Great Poet, as

I explain in the poem: not our *best* poet because, of course, that was Shakespeare, but he was next, he was the runner-up. So I had the admiration for poetry at home, though nobody ever read any, but it *was* important – the atmosphere was there. Then of course with the Plymouth Brethren I had hymns, which, in that they are devotional in intention, are hardly ever very good poetry, but all the same there's something about the act of communication by rhyme and rhythm that sets one thinking about this way of conveying ideas. But I was very lucky at school: I had very good English teachers, and I was about eight when I decided to be a poet.

Is that so? But you actually started quite late as a serious adult poet.

Oh yes. There was a great gulf. When I was a child I wrote poetry very fluently. I crammed the school magazines with my effusions. But when I left school and went to university, and particularly when I went to live abroad, I wasn't living in the right sort of atmosphere and, when I looked round, it seemed as though poetry had gone and had departed with childish things. It seemed to have gone away with my childish experiences and not come in with my adult ones. But then quite by accident, I fell in with some poets and in a spirit of not very edifying emulation I thought, 'Well, if they can do it, I can,' and proceeded to do so.

When you started doing that, what sort of influences were there for you to emulate?

Oh, most unfortunate. They were nearly the death of me, poetically. I'd been living abroad and when I got back to England…it was in the Fifties, it's true, but poetry was still in thrall to the techniques of the Forties. That carried on quite a long time. It was just before the coming of the Movement, which would have given me better models and much more interesting standards. It was really the decline of the poetry of the Forties and I simply fell under its sway. What I'd been doing when I was abroad was mostly not sitting reading poetry. I'd been enjoying myself in a way I wasn't allowed to when I was a child and poetry reading hadn't come into it much: I'd no idea what had been going on. And so all this lush, lavish, rather vague approach was a very dangerous influence for someone who ought not, at the age of 28, to have been a beginner, but I was starting all over again and was particularly vulnerable to this kind of thing – and not the best of it, the worst of it.

What helped you to get over the fever?

Unkind critics mostly. I was really influenced by what they said, and some people said some very ferocious things. But of course by this time it was too late to join in with the Movement, and then at the beginning of the Sixties I thought, 'Well, I will try something plainer,' and then the critics said it was too plain and after that I thought: 'Well, I'll just write what I feel like. It's not just that you can't please everybody, you can't please *anybody*, so just go ahead.' And that was a liberating moment.

In your third book, Just like the Resurrection, *it's very noticeable not only that the metres get looser but also that the subject matter becomes more mundane. Did those things go together for you? I mean, was it a revolution in yourself?*

It was, and I think where it really showed itself was when I stopped using quite so many similes and started using metaphor, which is obviously so much stronger. That was why I kept so many pieces out of the *Collected Poems*, which as you said was severely edited. That was one of the reasons why I severely edited it: everything was like something else – in a way that life isn't. So I cast out the similes and turned to much stronger metaphors. I think that was where the two things came together – subject matter and technique.

What were your models for loosening your technique? I mean, how did you learn to move away from rigid metrical paradigms to looser forms?

Oh, wide reading in the twentieth century and of course in poets like Hopkins who started loosening the traditional metres long before, though he wasn't known about until well into the twentieth century. By reading others: not in any way to imitate, because in fact I was incapable of imitating the best of the writers of free verse, but at least to see that such things were possible.

Do you consider that you ever write free verse in fact?

Oh yes, I do. Some of it's meant to be free verse, but I would be the first to admit that it is not the thing I do best. I find it very difficult to do what you have to do with really good free verse and that is create, originate, a rhythm in your own head and then follow it. I could do one or the other but not the two together and that has to be done. You know, the old thing about playing tennis without the net – I think I need a net.

So what nets do you use? You no longer write in rigid forms, so what alternatives are there?

I try to take traditional forms and make them more flexible, make them less of a stranglehold. With regard to rhyme, I love rhyme, but I try to avoid full-rhyme. (Or I have done up to now: I'm thinking of returning to it.) I think it was probably the hymns that did that, you see, with their thumping rhythms and their inflexible rhyme-schemes – you know, often ABAB in a tiny little quatrain.

You mentioned Hopkins. Hopkins is not obviously present in your work as an influence, so what does he mean to you exactly?

He means a great many very complicated things – technically and from the point of view of subject matter. As he explains in that rather impenetrable introduction – but I think I see what he means at the end – he was basically taking traditional forms but introducing a syncopation into them, so that they didn't come out as mid-nineteenth-century poetry tended to come out when it was getting a little bit tired and weary and was not in the hands of the masters. I saw how he did that and rejoiced: it seemed to make so many things possible but although one could parody a Hopkins poem very easily, one couldn't imitate it. Not possibly I think – it's all or nothing.

So you derive from it some notion of movement...

Precisely. And movement rather than rhythm. The poems *move* and if only I could get some of mine moving in that way, I would be very happy indeed. And of course another thing is the rhyme. I use half-rhyme because I have a certain timidity (based on the childhood regiment of hymns) about full-rhyme, though I'm hoping to pluck up enough attack to go back to it quite soon. But Hopkins's rhymes are *outrageous*; if you just look at the ones in 'Felix Randal', they're outrageous – and yet the poem is written at such white heat that you're quite unconscious of them.

Another thing in Hopkins, I suppose, is that he has such a strong sense of physical landscape...

Yes indeed, that is true, which is also my attitude and it's one of the reasons why I'm so happy living in Devon.

You obviously have very strong roots in Devon; you obviously feel some sort of allegiance.

Yes. For many of the middle years of my life, I was afraid that it was something sentimental and contrived – a sign of getting old and, you know, that's what people do. But having thought that one over and not bothered too much about it, I'm sure that there's much more to it than that. I think it's something much more real, much more tough and much more precise. There's a kind of sharpness, a kind of asperity, about Hopkins's poetry which one would indeed try to emulate. It's this whole question of precision; it's a *hard* sort of poetry, it's not these awful wispy little longings after the eternal, or anything like that. Probably it's the nature of his own conviction. I hope I've got this right: when an interviewer asked Jung did he think there was a God, he said: 'No, I don't *think*. I *know*.' And Hopkins is like that – he doesn't think, he doesn't even believe, he just knows.

Are you yourself a particularly religious person?

Yes, I think I am in a certain way. I don't think I could do without it, simply because I *haven't* done without it. Most people who leave a fundamentalist religion tend to leave religion for good, but I couldn't, and why I know I couldn't is that I didn't. I can't say that I move around in a sort of whirlpool of devotion. I feel as anybody does who's left the Plymouth Brethren: I feel very relaxed. But I don't know if that really would describe what you would mean by a religious person. It probably wouldn't. It sounds a bit negative really.

It's just that when I read the poems I find religious preoccupations to be insistent themes. But I also find almost a mistrust of religion in the poems, or rather a mistrust of that part of yourself that might lead you into being religiose.

Yes, I have a horror of fervour. I have a *horror* of it. It's having a physical reaction on me as I speak. The sheer idea of it. But then, you see, that's a fundamentalist upbringing for you.

When one reads through the Collected Poems, *there's a particular image that comes up very frequently, which is that of witches. There's an early poem called 'Witch', there's quite a recent poem called 'Mighty, Mighty Witches: Salem, Mass.' and there are several others. What does that image mean for you?*

Benevolence. And I don't mean that I'm making the silly distinction between white witches and black witches. No, to me they convey a sort of benevolence, and strength of course – and not exactly protectiveness. I don't think they are dear old ladies or anything like that really – much misunderstood. I think they're just what they're made out to be but I can't help feeling ultimate goodwill in them.

I just wondered whether this had something to do with feminism, perhaps? Perhaps that's the wrong word for it, but is it something to do with a woman's kind of spirituality?

Yes, as a matter of fact I'd never thought of that. I'm a rather wonky feminist, but I do think that I find something maternal in witches. Yes, I do think so. And that perhaps has various implications.

And how does feminism affect the writing of poetry? It always seems to me that poetry has been, over the centuries, so much a man's art that it must sometimes be difficult for women to slot into it.

If you mean, as I expect you do, is there any real difference between the sort of poetry that women write and that men write, I can't see there is, but a number of people whose opinions I respect say you could tell at once. *I* can't. You know I had occasion to read a few days ago Charlotte Brontë's remarks about Emily Brontë's poetry. She says that Emily wrote in a manner which was not considered feminine, and then she goes on to talk about Anne, and I don't think she makes the connection in her own mind, but she answers the question by saying that Anne's poetry on the contrary had 'a sweet sincerity'. So that's what women's poetry has, according to Charlotte Brontë: it has a sweet sincerity. I don't think that applies to the twentieth century. I think at least we've grown out of sweet sincerity.

I particularly wondered, thinking of witches again, whether women poets need to adopt roles or personae which are different from the ones that men use.

Oh, they certainly do need to adopt them. It really goes back to your earlier question: how I had to alter my work very much to begin with. I was always expressing myself as Leda or Juliet or Clytemnestra or Brünnhilde or something. I had to get out of that! But I still think that, if it is done in a way where the essence of what you are trying to say perhaps about yourself comes across, I see no reason why not. I don't write many personal poems; I've never been a confessional poet and at my age I'm not likely to start now. In the days when confessional poetry was the only thing to do I did suffer very badly in general lack of acclaim, because I wasn't telling anybody anything that I didn't choose to tell them.

But you do touch some painful and sensitive areas in the poems. I'm particularly conscious of how often your poems seem to talk about death, without being in any way morbid. What strikes me about it is that I suspect it's almost the motive behind the poems for you. Is that possible?

Oh yes. That, if I may say so, is a very shrewd remark, because when I was a child I was more terrified of dying than other children – if one could judge from their conversation, which probably one couldn't. I did seem to be abnormally terrified of dying. I used to think I had all sorts of dreadful illnesses and wouldn't be living in time much longer, and eternity didn't sound too happy a state of affairs. I was terrified. But then it occurred to me – this was when I was eight – that if I could become a great poet, perhaps somebody would put bulletins up on the railings of some great building to say that I was sinking fast or, you know, 'She is no better, she is much the same'! Something like that, some comment. And I felt that, if the eyes of the world were on me, I could bear it. Of course I don't think that now, but that was my childish remedy, because I wanted to do something about it, to fight back, and so I thought, well, words are the only thing I'm any good at: I'm never likely to be a great singer or a great high-jumper or anything of that sort at all, and indeed I never have been, but I knew I was clever with words, and so a poet.

London, 9 May 1990
(Broadcast: 2 June 1990)

Charles Causley

Among our more prominent contemporary poets, Charles Causley stands almost alone as being what once upon a time poets always were: a maker of songs. I say *songs* because most of his poems, even if not actually meant to be sung, are in song form: they are ballads, chants, carols, riddles, shanties and nursery rhymes. He is a *maker* of songs in the grand Old English sense of the word: a craftsman who sees his job as the production of well-wrought artefacts. It follows from this that, when the poet speaks *in propria persona*, he does so not in order to draw attention to himself, but because there is no other way to address the subject in hand.

Or that always seemed to be the case. Latterly, Causley has given in to the sometimes painful process of exploring his own memories in quieter, more meditative forms. This is particularly so in his most recent books: *Secret Destinations* (1984) and *A Field of Vision* (1988).

Causley was born in Cornwall, where he still lives, in 1917. He began working in modest clerical jobs. What changed his life fundamentally was service in the Navy during the war, when in spite of the fears and discomforts – or perhaps because of them – he began writing poetry. For most of his life since then he has been a school-teacher and a hugely productive man of letters. Not surprisingly, his *Collected Poems* (1975) is dominated by Cornwall, the sea, childhood and echoes of war.

Did you write anything before you joined the Navy?

Oh yes, I did. When I was about five years old, I wrote a novel set in the West End of London with a lot of lords and ladies in it. I always wanted to be a writer. I'm not quite sure what sort of writer I wanted to be, but I wrote and wrote as a little boy – as a tiny boy and while I was at school – and when I was in my teens I wrote and published plays. I even wrote a radio play and thought it was rather remarkable until I heard some really good ones. Oh yes, it wasn't just the war – but it was the war, it was being in the Navy, that channelled me into writing *poems*.

How did that come about? I mean, why the Navy?

It was because nobody had told me that in the English literary tradition it's quite impossible to be both a poet and a novelist and a playwright. One must be one thing *or* the other. Very few people have succeeded in doing the lot, or people of the sort of ability that I had, anyway. And if you're stuck on a mess deck, living on the mess deck of a destroyer or a corvette with eighty other people in a very small space, you *can't* write a play or a novel, but you can write poems in your head while you're doing boring, repetitive jobs and that's exactly what happened to me. I can't imagine a situation where I haven't got something or other going on inside my head in the way of a poem or whatever.

What were your first models at that time? Were you imitating anyone?

Not consciously. I was a child of the Thirties. I left school in my sixteenth year, didn't go to University, went straight into working in an office. So I relied on learning about poetry from reading literary weeklies. I mean weeklies like the old *New Statesman*, and literary journals like *Horizon*, and John Lehmann's *New Writing* and all that. I was always extremely interested and, through reading such papers, I became familiar with the work of Day Lewis, of MacNeice, of Spender and particularly of Auden. Auden impressed me tremendously, because Auden spoke as a poet in warning tones. We knew what was going to happen, we knew what Hitler was up to – the newspapers told us all lies, but the poets, in my view, told the truth.

Am I right in thinking that the experience of the Thirties and the war is a kind of backdrop to a great deal of what you write even now?

Oh very much so, very much so. I mean I still remember anniversaries and things that happened – not always desperately thrilling things. War on the whole is a very boring process, except for about five minutes each year – unless you're very, very unlucky, and I was very lucky. But I can never put it out of my mind and never forget what happened and what might happen again. Of course this was underpinned by my father's experience; my father was a late casualty of the First World War. I can hardly remember my father at all; he was a soldier who died in 1924 finally – he was invalided home from France – and it was through reading poems of Wilfred Owen and Sassoon and so forth that I got some kind of inkling as a very young man, as a schoolboy, as to what might have happened to my father and what the war might have been like for him. It always seems to have been a kind of backdrop to my life, right up to 1947, when the war was over.

I'm struck by the fact, as indeed most people who write about your work are, that you have such an affinity with the ballad form and I wonder where that came from. Was it something to do with being in the Navy?

Well, it might have been; it was all an accident. I mean I had no academic training: my reading was totally unguided. I remember an academic saying to me that quite clearly I'd studied the whole thing. Not at all, not at all. What really happened, as far as I was concerned, was that I thought the ballad was an extremely difficult form. I still think it is: it's very difficult to be simple or to seem simple and it presented a very interesting and absorbing and difficult problem which I felt had to be solved.

It's interesting that you say it's difficult to be simple, because a lot of people think of the ballad as being simple, in fact possibly even simplistic. To me, the surface of your poems is simple, but the poems underneath the surface are complex. How do you achieve that?

I don't really know. Of course, I've no intention whatever that they should be simplistic. I remember when I began teaching very young children I could never find poems to *read* to them. I tried to read A.A. Milne and they were really bored out of their minds, and so was I. Then one day I went into the classroom and I took the wrong set of books and I'd got on the top a collection of English and Scottish ballads edited by Robert Graves. And this was a crowd of about forty rather tough little Cornish boys who I certainly shouldn't leave behind in the classroom while I got the right books, so I just opened it and started to read one of the ballads. It really worked: they understood *all* the implications. It taught me how very sophisticated children can be in their apprehension of what goes on in a poem. They knew all about the coinage of the ballad; they knew all about betrayal and illegitimacy and family disasters – all these things that happen but which we didn't really talk about in school in those days. I could see that they were going along with me. And I think that was very important to me because I could see that with a ballad, if you were lucky and if you worked hard enough, you could do almost anything, as long as you observe *the* most important rule of all: don't go on too long!

Ballads are elliptical, aren't they? They leave a lot to the imagination...

Yes, absolutely. The ballad is like a film. Each stanza should be like a frame and it jumps from one to the other and there's a wonderful sort of gap in between, across which some kind of electric spark has to jump. You have to make it look that way and the business of compressing it down and down and down is to me extremely difficult and very, very absorbing. But then it's the same with poetry generally; I mean it's true, for me anyway, that the poem should use the least number of words possible. I always knock out far more words than ever exist on the page at the end. I think a poem's like a little pile of cards, a little house made of cards, and if you take out one more word the whole structure should collapse: nothing too much, nothing too little. Very difficult, very interesting. That's why writers trip over paving-stones and walk into walls.

Do you think there was something about the ballad that was also part of the atmosphere of the 1940s?

Now you come to mention it, I think that's probably true, but it was unconscious in my scheme of things. It could be seen that one thought one was playing a part in some gigantic kind of pattern, but not at all. I suppose writing for me was in one way a kind of retreat – I could retreat, get right inside myself and try and analyse and write about what was happening, which was something totally strange and exotic and entirely different from anything that had happened to me before. Up to 1940, I wouldn't have dreamed of writing poems about the curious characters who haunted the little market town where I lived. I thought the subject of poetry was away and somewhere else and I had to go there to find it. Nobody told me that poetry is underneath your nose – it's happening there all the time. It took me a long time to find that out – too long.

That's interesting, because there's a lot about travel in your poetry, isn't there? I mean is that to do with going to look for it?

Oh no, one never goes to look. No, if you look for a subject, you'll never find it. It has to come round the corner like an unexpected 88 bus and knock you down, and you're picking yourself up and dusting yourself off and the experience suddenly resolves itself into something. But one should never look for it.

I sometimes get the feeling that the traditions you plug into as a writer, particularly the ballad, are slightly subversive traditions. I mean that in a sense you're not writing high art; you're attempting slightly to undermine that concept. Would that be true?

Yes, yes, yes, I would hope so. I mean the poet has almost got to be a bit of a saboteur. I don't admire saboteurs all that amount but I don't know anybody who's been killed by a poem, so one merely hopes for the best. But there's a good tradition of that kind of poet, you know.

And the other thing is that it obviously connects with a religious side of yourself as well, which I suppose reminds one to some extent of William Blake: that combination of the traditional form being used for subversion on the one hand and the visionary aspect on the other. Is that something you're conscious of?

Not any more than I can help. The phoney William Blake figure, with the straws in the hair and all that, is something I find really rather trying. One simply tries to speak as one finds in the way that John Clare most certainly did and still does of course...it's a voice that still goes on, still resounds...But I'm not absolutely sure about my position as a religious poet, though some people call me that. I wouldn't call myself a Christian – I have a Christian background, brought up as a little Church of England choirboy and Sunday School boy and all that. And the Old Testament stories have always fascinated me and when it's possible to marry them to a twentieth-century attitude... For example, the German poet Karen Gershon, Jewish poet, who came over here in the 1930s as a child and lost both her parents in the Holocaust – never saw them after she came over here in I think it was 1938: she was first able to write about the Holocaust through the mesh of the Old Testament religious stories like Lot's wife, the Exodus and all that. Now that really is quite wonderful, I think, and it's a kind of continuing strand that poets have been able to latch on to and keep going, and I think it's very difficult to write what's called a religious poem in a twentieth-century context. But it is just possible and I certainly try to do so, but not always with very great success.

One does get the feeling, as one reads through your Collected Poems, *that you move slowly away from the ballad. When did you first become conscious that you were doing that?*

Well, you know, I was quite surprised to be dubbed a ballad writer at all. I just wrote what I thought were very simple poems like 'The Nursery Rhyme of Innocence and Experience':

> I had a silver penny
> And an apricot tree
> And I said to the sailor
> On the white quay

And I didn't really get worried until I started getting letters, particularly from America, saying, 'Dear Mr Causley, What did you mean when you said "I had a silver penny"?' Well, I meant I had a silver penny!

People will not believe that you mean what you say!

That's right!

But certainly in your last two books, and probably earlier than the last two books, the forms are much less insistently musical and constructed.

Yes, that's true. I think a lot of my earlier poems are overwritten. I certainly think that a poem needs to have music in it. Not too much, but it has to have a musical line in order that people might remember it. How can you remember a poem unless you have something to latch on to like a rhythm or, in my case, a musical line? But it mustn't be too insistent. A tremendous number of my poems have been set to music – almost always disastrously, because I think there might be too much music in them already. I've written many works for music theatre now, librettos and so forth – one has to be careful not to inject too much music into the lines, because the composer has to have an area in which to operate. And I feel that I must draw away from that sort of excessively lyrical tone. It can become too sugary. I don't admire a lot of my early poems at all nowadays.

Did you at some point make a decision to move away from all that?

Yes, about ten or eleven years ago. I still get the ballad thing sort of hung around my head, and that's very nice and very attractive. I write books for children, or they're called children's books, but when I write a poem I don't know whether it's for a child or an adult, I just write the poem and, if it works out, if it seems to work out, and if it seems to me that a child could cotton on to most of what was happening in the poem, well then that's a children's poem, because a children's poem must be one that works for the adult as well as the child, not just the child. It isn't a kind of suit of clothes which a child, when it's fourteen years old, can throw away. You carry a poem for the rest of your life, hopefully, so I would write a poem and if I thought children could understand it, I'd put it into a file called 'children's poems' and publish it in a children's book. But when I come to make my *Selected Poems*, or my *Collected*, then I wouldn't really worry where the poem came from originally – whether it was what was called a children's book or whether it was an adult's book, and in the end it becomes smoothed over and nobody seems able really to tell the difference.

Take a book like Early in the Morning, *which is a book of nursery rhymes – in other words a book which is readable by really quite young children. Do you mean that in writing those poems you are unaware of the fact that they are suitable for one audience rather than another?*

Yes, I don't concern myself about the audience at all. It's no good thinking about the reader over your shoulder, whether it's a child or an adult – especially a child. Terrifying things children: I taught too long to think anything other than that...I mean, yes, you have to shut all that out and just write the poem, work away at it, and see if it works or not. Never ask anybody else's opinion. I would never dream of doing that. I regard anybody who thrusts a poem in my hand and says 'What do you think of that?' as making an improper suggestion. You have to make the decision yourself. People are too polite to tell you it doesn't work, or they don't know, or whatever – it's a very embarrassing kind of question. You have to decide on whether the thing more or less works, or not. But I've never written anything that I've totally admired, not by a very long chalk. That's why one goes on writing, always hoping that the next one is going to be the one perfect piece. God knows when that'll be!

London, 2 July 1990
(Broadcast: 5 July 1990)

Craig Raine

It sometimes befalls the aspiring young poet that he writes a poem so characteristic of his work as a whole that he is saddled with its fame for the rest of his career. It happened to Yeats with 'The Lake Isle of Innisfree', to Larkin with 'Church Going' and to Gunn with 'On the Move'; and it looks as though it has happened to Craig Raine with the title poem of his 1979 collection, *A Martian Sends a Postcard Home*, which has fathered a whole school of lesser Martians. Its manner was already present in his first book, *The Onion, Memory*, which appeared in 1978. The poems in both collections are built around ingenious, unlikely and instantly memorable metaphors: a dead woman's nipples are 'patches from a cycle kit', light-switches stare 'like flat-faced barn-owls', a child's milk-teeth are 'segments of sweet-corn'.

When his next book, *Rich*, appeared in 1984, it became clear that Raine had moved on. The new poems reflect on the method's deficiencies, while at the same time reaffirming his belief in the plenitude of the world and the richness of the imagination. He went on to experiment with verse drama: there is an opera libretto, *The Electrification of the Soviet Union*, and a play, *1953*, which is adapted from Racine's *Andromaque*. There is prose too: a book of essays, *Haydn and the Valve Trumpet*, and at the centre of *Rich* an evocative memoir in praise of his parents, who were northern, working class and, by anyone's standards, strikingly out of the ordinary.

In that memoir in Rich, *you in effect attribute your creative instincts to your father – boxer, raconteur, showman and medium. But you don't say how this creativity first got funnelled into poetry. When did you first start reading it?*

I suppose when I was fourteen, at school: we were read some Betjeman – 'The Subaltern's Love Song'. I suppose I was struck by that, and then Prufrock. 'The Love-Song of J. Alfred Prufrock' is what most people have as their first experience of poetry – it's the first poem they go to bed with. These were the first two things. After that I started to read poetry, but read it in that sort of blind adolescent way that people have where they simply don't understand how something works. It's a little like watching television and seeing pictures on the screen and thinking: I could do something vaguely like that. But it's years before you (as it were) get round the back and take the back of the set off and see how the tube and the electrics actually work, so that you can make something roughly comparable yourself. I don't think I really understood poetry – though I enjoyed it in a strange purblind way – until I was 22 or something like that. Of course, as soon as you get real direct pleasure, you can start translating this into writing. As far as my parents go, I think my mother is as important as my father. What I get from my father, I think, is a huge gift for exaggeration and what I get from my mother is a complete respect for the literal truth. What I try to do in my work is somehow to bring these two different genetic imperatives to bear on the subject matter I'm dealing with.

Who were the literary models then, apart from your parents as life-models?

Well, of course one always has them. In my case, perfectly straight-forwardly, the first poet I really read with deep pleasure and under-standing was Ted Hughes. I don't think it shows very much because I don't write about animals. I mean, I'm just cunning enough to avoid the obvious trap. But he was an enormous influence. You can see he's got a tremendous image-making power – he uses simile like no-one else – and clearly one was ravished by this. I think the other great influence was Lowell, whom I was very keen on for a time – and still am in some ways – but the real thing that transformed my life was reading *Ulysses* by Joyce and seeing that you could write about any-thing and, if you were really intelligent enough and gave it enough thought and attention, buying a kidney at a butcher's shop could be one of the most interesting things you could read about.

How did that come over into poetry – Joyce's prose?

Very simply, in the sense that having read him on Leopold Bloom going into a butcher's shop and buying a kidney and sliding 'the moist tender gland' into his pocket, laying his coins 'on the rubber prickles' to be read and then trickled into the till, I thought: Well, let's do this with a grocer. You simply go into competition and that's what you have to do as a writer. I know it sounds hubristic, but that's precisely what you do. You think: If he can do it, I can do it. And also, because you're going from prose to poetry, the element of theft involved here is less obvious.

When did it first strike you that metaphor was so overwhelmingly important to you?

I think because I use metaphor anyway. Clearly what I liked about Hughes and what I liked about Lowell was that they used metaphor and used it very well and very boldly and effectively. But I think actually what was happening was that they were speaking to something that was already there in me. Hopkins is somebody else I admire enormously and, when I'm talking in a relaxed non-studio mood and I'm flying (as it were) in conversation, I use metaphors all the time. My friends will tell you that I'm a very unfair man in argument because this is the way I argue – from one metaphor to the next and, of course, they're notoriously slithery.

Perhaps we could pursue that a little. There's something that strikes me as especially slithery about the way that you link metaphors in a poem. In 'A Martian Sends a Postcard Home', for instance: the poem begins with the Martian talking about books but he doesn't know what books are, but then later in the poem he talks about mist and he says it makes the world look 'dim and bookish', so there's a kind of play there on the audience somehow pretending to be ignorant of what is really going on.

I don't see why you find this so difficult, Clive. Were a real Martian to come down and write something, we wouldn't be able to understand a word of it because none of us speak Martian! Clearly what you have here is a perfectly straightforward convention of the kind that you have in war films. In war films, the English people speak English and the Germans speak broken English – they don't speak German. It's a kind of convention – that's all.

I'm not actually saying I find it difficult. What I'm really asking you is whether you, in doing that, are trying to draw the reader's attention to the process of reading.

I suppose everything one writes does that. No, the form of 'A Martian Sends a Postcard Home' is the form of a postcard. We're all familiar with sonnets and couplets and odes and irregular odes, but it's possible to write a poem in a form that hasn't been used before, in this case the form of a postcard. Everybody writes a postcard saying: 'Uncle Willy fell in the sea. Weather's been terrible for days. Lodgings not bad. See you next week. Wish you were here.' In other words, it's an excuse for very, very heterogeneous subject-matter. But also it begins with a misunderstanding of reading – 'Caxtons are mechanical birds' – and it ends with people sleeping together and dreaming, which the Martian thinks is reading about themselves. So the poem actually closes on itself with two views of reading and, if you want to go back to the business about 'bookish' – 'If he doesn't understand about books how does he know "bookish"?' – the answer is that 'bookish' is an adjective which doesn't necessarily refer to books. So that logically I can argue my way out of this corner but I don't particularly want to, since it seems to me that we're being over-literal. You're just expected to float from one thing to the next. 'Slithery' if you like. I just say: less ponderous. There's no point in arraigning this poem before a court of law and saying 'In the twenty-fifth stanza, my boy' – tugging at my barrister's gown – 'in the twenty-fifth stanza you said such and such, whereas in the twelfth stanza you said this.' It's much frailer as a work of art than that and, if you do that to it, it will just burst into tears in the witness box. Now you have an example of me talking in metaphor, very unfairly, but this is what I do!

Why I asked you the question was really that it's pretty clear from the more recent work that one of the things you're doing is looking at language. You've written this series of theses called 'Babylonish Dialects', which is about the subject of idiolects, and in certain poems in Rich *you draw your readers' attention to what language does by using languages which are unfamiliar to them.*

Yes, I invented some languages. It seems to me that, if you invent a language, it's yet another way of making the world seem new. You actually alter the way that people think. I mean: 'skinhead'. Now it's lost all of its quality but the person who coined that in the first instance was a genius – it is an absolutely brilliant little phrase. So the first person who said it and the first person who heard it must have had the tops of their heads taken off. 'Skinhead'. Brilliant. Then they tell it to everybody and, in the end, it gets worn out. Wittgenstein says that language is like a crumpled piece of silver paper. We can never quite, however much we try, straighten it out and make it completely fresh all the time, so therefore you have to change the language and that's why it's useful to invent new language: a form of pidgin, a kind of Siamese or whatever it is – I use a sort of Elizabethan at one point in *Rich*. All to this purpose: to refresh the palate and refresh the ear.

Can we take the poem you mention that's written in pidgin, the poem called 'Gauguin'? There is an obvious analogy between the way that poem works and the way the most elaborate of the Martian metaphors work, which is that the reader is just for a while held at a distance, the distance of incomprehension, and has to apply some ingenuity to the poem. Then suddenly the poem 'gives' to him or her.

I think this is right. But don't you think this is true of all good poetry? There are very few words in a poem. Say there are fifty – for a prose writer this is absolutely nothing. Now what these fifty words have to do is entice you into them and then surround you and then start stroking you and tying you up and locking you in, so you find it very hard to leave because you're having such a good time or you can't find the door. You're into the poem, but where's the door that lets you out of the poem? Somehow you have to trap people there so that they will give these words the benefit of their proper attention. The way we read these days! We read like a bloody 125 – zoooom! And that's it. All the pages are going like this on the edge of the platform. We have to slow down for poetry and poetry has to slow us down by trapping us, holding us, tugging at our sleeve, buttonholing us, giving us a good big kiss.

But the point I'm trying to make is that you slow us down slightly more than some other writers do and you deliberately baffle the reader – temporarily. I'm not trying to suggest that your poems are obscure, because they're not – and indeed there are poets I can think of who are much more difficult and much more obscure but who aren't actually trying to baffle the reader. But in your case, it seems to me, you want to temporarily baffle the reader, so that there's this experience of 'give'. That's my own experience as a reader of the poems.

What you want to do is turn the reader into a poet. So that you don't say: 'Here it is on a plate, this is this.' You say: 'Here's this and this and this' – and they're left with a problem. They solve it and, in solving it, they get the pleasure of being in your position. You don't actually do it for them. You sort of set the thing up, so that, if they're reading properly, they can only get to the answer, but they get to the answer walking themselves. Who was it said about the Woolworth's heiress: 'too rich to walk'? Readers have to walk! I'm not going to carry them to the lines and say: 'Here it is'. My poems are not drips either. They have to walk around and see it for themselves. If they don't understand something in my poems, it's always a good idea to go outside and look at it. You know, I say that baby-teeth are like sweet-corn. Somebody once said to me at a reading, 'But teeth are white and sweetcorn's yellow', and I said, 'Why don't you just go and look at a bit of sweetcorn and look at a tooth?' Check it out! Then you'll find out that people aren't looking any more and they aren't reading any more and the way I write is a way of making sure that they do. It's just slowing people down. Making them pay attention.

There are certain immensely simple poems of Ezra Pound's that I know you admire and I wonder if we can make a comparison and contrast here. Pound thinks he can renew our sense of the world simply by naming things – by simply indicating, say, two oxen beyond the roadway. You seem to think that it has to be done by extraordinary, roundabout analogies.

There are two ways of doing it and Pound has both of them. Pound's an Imagist – you know, the Metro:

> The apparition of these faces in the crowd;
> Petals on a wet, black bough.

The thing being described, then the image. I mean this is round the houses. What he does in the Chinese poems, which are the most simple, is he invents a style. Now this seems to me to be a particularly interesting thing to do. I mean, in his other poems he can use extraordinary elaborate words: 'macerations' – that kind of word. You get no words like this in his Chinese poems. They're absolutely pared-down and made simple, every line is end-stopped, they're kind of rhythmically inscrutable, hardly an adjective in sight, bang-bang-bang, fact-fact-fact and, yes, he names things. He names the apricot-boughs and the peach-boughs, but he will also (even better) name places – Cho-fu-Sa, or whatever it is – and you think: This is amazing. How does this work? Actually, that's incredibly devious. It's not as straightforward as it seems, because we've no idea where this place is, where it might be. It just speaks to us like music really and I think that this is a very conscious effort on his part to be simple. What he's using there is the rhetoric of plainness. Now plainness is a rhetoric just like any other – it's a technique which one can use. Indeed, to speak for myself, I used it absolutely consciously when I wrote an opera because I know that only one word in seven travels across the lights, because you've got the band in between and the singers are distorting the words, so you have to use a simple medium. It's terrific fun, but it's not the only way to do it.

What use do you make of the sorts of criticism that are made of your work? I mean, you have come in for a great deal of criticism from one quarter or another. You've been accused, for instance of trivialising the world, degrading your own subject matter.

It would be so nice, wouldn't it, just to say: 'You're absolutely right: my entire aim is to trivialise the world'? At least we could agree about that. Well, obviously I don't think this and what one sees in the history of criticism is that it's always the same: whenever new writers come along they're told that they're clever and they're heartless and that their cleverness gets in the way of the world. This has happened practically since the first Neanderthaler chipped a sonnet on the cave wall! What you expect is that people will stop saying 'Speak for the heart!', which is what they're always telling you, by which they mean some horrible, pludgy, emotional equivalent of a Cornetto. Now, if you take someone like Eliot – there's a wonderful prose-poem of his called 'Hysteria', which is about a woman having hysterics. What is wonderful about this poem is that Eliot has no compassion for her, he doesn't care about her, what he wants to do is control the afternoon. Now anyone who's ever been with a hysterical woman – or a hysterical man for that matter – knows that this is what you feel like. You don't think: This is a tragedy, or I love her anyway, or I love him anyway. At the actual time you're thinking: 'If we could just salvage "some of the fragments of the afternoon"', and Eliot is absolutely true to this emotion and it's a perfectly good emotion to feel. People who say 'Have a heart' mean: 'Have *my* heart. Have the heart that we all share. Be Bob Geldof.' I don't want to be Bob Geldof. I want to be able to have the freedom just to like some things and to dislike some other things. Listen: poetry has world-rights on eloquence. This is what it does better than anything else. It also often has world-rights on exaggeration. Now exaggeration I'm not interested in. Genuine eloquence I am interested in. But exaggeration, particularly exaggeration of what one feels, disgusts me. And English poetry is full of it, particularly now. You just want to throw up. Nearly every book you get hold of, it's some terrible middle-class poet saying how wonderful people in the pub are. You know, they're *real* people! As if the person who wrote the poem wasn't real. There are many, many poems like this in English poetry and we could do with fewer of them.

London, 23 July 1990
(Broadcast: 5 August 1990)

Seamus Heaney

Seamus Heaney probably reaches a larger public than any poet now writing in the English language. An Ulsterman by birth, he has made his home in the Irish Republic for more than twenty years. He also teaches four months a year at Harvard University and was until recently Professor of Poetry at Oxford. He has become, as few poets do, a figure on the international scene. There has been talk lately of a kind of poetic diaspora: in the post-colonial era, it is said, the centres of English poetry are no longer New York or London. Perhaps in our post-modern world there are no centres anyway.

Yet one thinks of Heaney as a profoundly local poet, rooted in the agricultural life of Northern Ireland, belonging to the Roman Catholic community, and taking his bearings from a way of life that was just beginning to give in to the modern world when he reached manhood. (He was born in 1939.) That world is celebrated in his first two books, but gives way in the next two to the darker roots of Irish history – notably in the so-called 'bog' poems from his 1975 collection *North*. For *North* registers the impact of the Troubles, which have been crucial to his poetry ever since.

Heaney has also been praised for his distinguished critical prose, for a fine translation from medieval Irish, *Sweeney Astray*, and for a verse-play, *The Cure at Troy*. But his own poetry remains the main concern. There have been four books since *North*: *Field Work* (1979), *Station Island* (1984), *The Haw Lantern* (1987) and, subsequent to this interview, *Seeing Things* (1991).

I get the feeling from your poems that you had a happy childhood. Is that true?

Yes, I would say my childhood was happy. I wasn't in any way made unhappy by the world I lived in. I mean, the circumstances in my home were secure and affectionate, and so were the circumstances of the world: the farm itself was our own land, we were among our own trees, our own fields and so on. So there was a sense of a completely trustworthy centre. But I suppose all children have a feeling of exile of some sort, a sense of strangeness – a faintly tragic sense of the world. So when I think of childhood, I also think of standing at the centre of a stillness, at a distance from things. I mean, I think everybody recollects their earliest life as somehow in the middle of a space that is separate and a little sorrowing.

Do you think that's especially true of children who are very verbal like yourself?

I don't know. I didn't become verbal until quite late on. There were three things in my life, I think, that animated me and brought me from a sense of fearfulness into some kind of confidence. Oddly enough, one of them was acting in a school play. I played the butler – *there's* a post-colonial symptom if you want it! – I played the butler in a play called *The Sport of Kings*. Somehow, crossing into that freedom, and a certain exultation in being applauded on the stage, and the fact that it's a different place and you aren't yourself, made it an important little moment. And then when I finished my degree at Queen's, I again got some kind of sense of being stamped and verified. And then, of course, starting to write, I suppose. All these things contributed to my being able to murmur on like this nowadays, but I do think of my early life as a little bit dumb and a little bit hampered, uneasy.

There's a sense in the early poems of speech being drawn out of silence. I wonder what the wellsprings of those poems really were.

I don't know. Obviously there was a kind of memory bank, just of the place and the things. But the household and the attitudes within the household where I grew up – and not just the household but the culture of rural Ulster, indeed Ulster generally – were suspicious of speech. The declaration of an emotion immediately made the emotion suspect – I think this is absolutely true of course! It was highly in place in our minds and in our dumb beings that the unspoken was the trustworthy, and the completely trustworthy exchange was the intuitive one, and the making explicit of the intuitive somehow vitiated it. I think poets especially feel some sympathy with that, because in some sense their project resides in that unspoken nub of intuition and potential.

The early poems with their silences tend to focus very much on things, the material facts of life, I think. Then in your third book, Wintering Out, *you start looking at language itself. I'm thinking particularly of poems like 'Broagh' and 'Anahorish'. There's also a feeling of mistrust for a language that, as an Irishman, you don't feel to be entirely yours.*

Wintering Out practised a kind of linguistic politics; it politicised language. It played with accepted conventional notions of Ulster culture, Irish history and so on. Because they are conventional doesn't mean that they aren't accurate. But this book was written between, say, '69 and '72, just at the moment of energy, revelation and danger. Revelation of a new possibility, the entry of a new danger in violence and the sense of change and the sense of reshaping – in a good way – the future of Ulster and Ireland. And in order to keep the energy running benignly and forward, rather than backward and malignly, I thought it better – and all of us did – not to mention the world of Ulster in terms of the old sectarian language, Protestant, Catholic, or whatever. So one way of acknowledging difference, and at the same time being true to one's own cultural attachments and stand-offs and so on, was to deal with language. Well, the plantation of Ulster obviously brings you English, and there's a certain pride in that the rural Ulster dialect has Elizabethan, Shakespearean pronunciations. That was one conventional theme the poems worked with. The other is that in rural Ulster also, in the place names, you have the Irish language present. You also have Scottish dialect words and so on. So the microscopic or slow-motion lingering on sounds and etymologies and so on was meant to be both a lyrical celebration of shared things and at the same time a pointer to differences. It was meant to be honest about division and at the same time to suggest that there was something in common, like the pronunciation of the [guttural] sound 'agh', which is difficult for, say, the 'southron' folk in England. I mean, the word 'Coagh', which I used to use to the telephone operators in London: they would say 'Oh, Co-ah'. So, the word 'Broagh', which is from the Irish word meaning a river bank – both Protestant and Catholic, Unionist and Nationalist, could say 'broagh'; they possessed that sound. So this was a frail, fragile, miniscule point of commonness, a point that was admittedly deep deep down in the speech, deep in the throat, deep in the hearth language.

The hopefulness implied in that particular strategy must have failed at some point, because certainly with North, *but already perhaps in* Wintering Out, *the violence forces its way into the poetry, doesn't it?*

Yes. Of course, the violence for people from Ulster was a manifestation of something that was always latent and potential. It's probably true to say that, for many people there, the violence was like a bad dream come true. It wasn't as big a surprise to them as it would have been for people on the British island looking across and saying 'My God, what's happening here?', because there had been a lot of smoothed-over danger in the Ulster situation; and people, particularly people on the Catholic side like myself, grew up resentful, with a strong sense, for example, of the RUC as a bruising symbol and actuality and with a sense of the truth of all the usual old cries of injustice about housing and promotions and jobs. So there was a sense of something suppressed and latent. But my own generation of Catholics perceived just that very emergence of themselves as a generation into the vocal world of the academy and the world of politics as an aspect of change itself. The fact that these things were now being protested about in politics and written about...So there was that amount of hope and trust in our generation that things were moving. Still, what happened over the four or five years of the Civil Rights and all that was that whatever was moving forward got driven back into the old places. I remember the Minister for Community Relations, a man called Dr Simpson from Antrim. (The Minister for Community Relations, incidentally, was only appointed when Community Relations went sky high! But that's another matter.) He said to me: 'You know, Seamus, your poems about our hay and spades and bogs and farms and all that, they are appreciated by both sides here, Protestants and Catholics. So, that just goes to prove that we really have, you know, a really trustworthy culture here.' And I thought to myself: Well, that's true, but if it's as consoling and verifying as that, giving us an escape from political realities, something else has to go into this poetry. And in a sense there *was*, after that, a deliberate sticking into it of more data and there was a blacker mood. Poetry hangs between civic hopes and just cruelly sticking your nose into what your deepest instinct tells you to. Sometimes you distrust poetry that relishes too much that sticking of the nose into the worst possibilities. On the other hand, I think you distrust more readily poetry that cheers too loudly for the good possibilities.

Are you thinking there of the 'bog' poems? Of a poem like 'Punishment', where you talk about understanding 'the exact / and tribal, intimate revenge'?

Yes. Well, I'm not thinking of any one poem in particular. I'm thinking of an attitude of being afraid of being too benign or too soothing. At the same time, of course, you don't want to say that nothing is possible. Those poems in *North*, for example: I suppose one should resay all this in this way – they weren't *quite* political poems, they weren't poems that sat down at the touchline of events and viewed the game and gave a report, they were *not* like that. They were written out of a kind of hutch, rather than a viewing box. And they were written when I was down in Wicklow, and I went to Wicklow *not* in order to escape the violence of the North or anything like that. I went to the place because I was thirty-two or three years of age and I had published three books which were well praised, but which I felt probably hadn't earned the praise that they got; I wanted to find out some trustworthiness in myself and in the enterprise of my own poetry. It was a writerly withdrawal, if you like, and there was a personal anxiety secluded in me – in County Wicklow, with my wife and two, then three, small children – and the anxiety of course drew itself from what was happening in the North; of course it did. But there was, if you like, an existential, personal tightness in the breast alone, and I think that those poems come out of that very tensed-up, hooped-up, closed-in mood; and like any poems, the 'bog' poems and so on were acts of momentary appeasement: stays against confusion, as Frost says. Obviously they had more to them than that but I would want to say that simple truth that all of us know: that poems of any personal need and intensity are personal before they are public or political.

I felt very strongly that The Haw Lantern *marked the first big change of direction since* North. *Is that what you felt yourself?*

I don't know about the direction. Certainly a change of mood, a change of pitch, a freedom to invent, a freedom to relish. I mean, there was something very surly in myself and in the poems in the title sequence of *Station Island*. I was reluctant to take pleasure in language. Language there is kind of shooting itself in the poetic foot, you know. And I think I'm glad to have done that, because one of the fears I have is of a too self-smiling lyricism, you know. But I feel now that the pleasures of the language itself and the sportiveness of inventing and just the simplicity of being whatever your volitions and impulses are – that they're enough to be going on with.

It seems to me that the pleasure now is in plainness rather than abundance. Is that right?

I developed this notion that the first poems I wrote were trying to be like stained glass but that I would like to write a poetry of window glass. And I found myself at a certain stage in my teaching in the late Seventies, when I was working at a Teacher Training College – in spite of all my old love for people like Hopkins and Keats, and that sort of richness – I found myself veering towards Wyatt and Marvell and the poetry of clarity and plain statement. Enjoying those short-beat lines of Yeats's in poems like 'The Fisherman' and so on. But still, when you are actually in the process of writing a poem, you aren't usually delivering policy statements to yourself about the kind of language you want to write. In general, I think the change may also be a matter of getting a bit older. The show-off element in diction and lingo – you start curbing that a bit.

What about the themes? I mean there are a number of parable poems in The Haw Lantern, *aren't there? And I get a feeling of a slightly more cosmopolitan atmosphere.*

That may be so. The parable poems came about as an accident. I wrote one which was commissioned by Amnesty; it was a poem called 'From the Republic of Conscience'. I had been reading and writing about people like Zbigniew Herbert and Holub and so on. And these parable poems were written in an assumed translatorese voice almost; they aren't my voice particularly – they are from an invented place. They were just a little riff in the middle of things. I don't see them as more or less than that. I don't see them as a way of proceeding. This whole 'cosmopolitan' thing and the idea of poetry at the margins somehow being at the centre and so on: that, as we know, is invented by people declaring that it is so. But I myself, I still feel I'm very much in Ireland. I know that my life has changed by being in the States; there has been a slight sense of eeriness and airiness in spending four months of the year in Cambridge, Massachusetts, flying on aeroplanes back and forth across the Atlantic. Jet-sitting, I call it, rather than jet-setting! But I think that that sense of slight airiness would come in your middle age anyway. I think that, in your late forties and early fifties, a certain self-absolution and freeing begins, and a certain disjunction from the verities of your twenties and thirties. So, I am not sure whether it's a matter of getting a little bit older or of travelling that bit more distance that has loosened the voice of the self over the years.

London, 2 August 1990
(Broadcast: 2 September 1990)

P.J. Kavanagh

I tend to think of P.J. Kavanagh as first and foremost a 'nature poet', very much in the tradition of Edward Thomas and Ivor Gurney. Neither Thomas nor Gurney was a 'modernist', but both of them 'modernised': they loosened the old metres, favoured conversational diction and sought to capture in words the exact texture and particularity of the things they so closely observed. Kavanagh has followed them in all these ways, and paid homage to both of them in two fine poems. He also edited the historic *Collected Poems of Ivor Gurney*, which for many of us, in 1982, re-adjusted our perspectives on modern poetry in England.

This is not to say that Kavanagh is stuck in a pre-war world of rural nostalgia, though there's plenty of evidence in his poems that he prefers the country to the city. It's rather that the vanishing countryside becomes for him a kind of vantage point from which to view our changing world, as well as the more general questions of human love and suffering that are always with us.

Born in 1931, Kavanagh has been a teacher overseas, a broadcaster and an actor, as well as what he now is, a professional writer, with six novels, two memoirs, some anthologies and a book of journalism to his credit. But the central focus of his work remains his poetry: seven books of it, now gathered together as *Collected Poems* (1992).

There's a very large autobiographical element in your work – indeed, you've also written a prose autobiography – so I'd like to start by talking about all that. I get the impression that your father was a great influence on your life and maybe on your work as a writer too. Is that right?

I certainly seem to recur to ideas of him. He was in a way – in a very genial and affectionate way – more or less an absentee father: he was out of the house most of the time and I was, anyway, mostly away at school. He lived by writing jokes and had a sort of quasi-rebellious attitude to society, as anybody who makes fun of things does. I think most people – or many *sons* anyway – live by reacting against the rigours and perhaps sternnesses of their father's view of the world. I couldn't react against him in that way and therefore he's always played a sort of nagging part in my consciousness.

The other person who seems to come up a lot, at least in your early writing, is your first wife, who died very suddenly when you'd only fairly recently been married. Looking back on it, do you think that loss, that suffering, helped to make you the artist that you are?

When I look at my own work, as I have had to do in order to construct these programmes, I am dismayed at the degree to which I appear to indulge in autobiography. But in answer to your question, it seemed to me almost at once that a personal loss of that magnitude must have some general significance. It must relate one to other people – rather than separate one from them – as an expression of the various experiences, glimpses, insights that it gave me. And to be expressed properly, they'd have to be expressed – because of the sort of writer I am – autobiographically: that gives them a kind of authenticity. In that way they would have general application. That's really, as I see now, how I've always worked. And yet the autobiographical element seems to me only superficial and, as I say, is meant to give the time and place, the authenticity, to the larger and more general feeling that I'm trying to share with others. That 'time and place' thing, I've recently discovered, is a very old Irish literary convention.

When I read through your poems from start to finish, I'm struck by how a poetic identity gradually develops and then hardens, becomes firm. The loss of your wife strikes me as one aspect of that. Another seems to be your move to the countryside. There's that fine long poem to your father about the move in About Time. *Why was that? How did moving to the country make such a substantial change to you as a poet?*

Well, again, when I go over my past work and I'm appalled by its autobiographical nature, I'm also appalled by the fact that I seem to have become at some stage a nature poet and my only answer to that is that one really doesn't choose. To some extent one is chosen. I was brought up in London. I always from my earliest years longed, absolutely longed – I think it was something to do with the Richmal Crompton 'William' stories – I longed to look at the bottom of ditches and go birds' nesting and so on (which I did at school actually). And as soon as the opportunity arose of being able to live in the country, I did – willy-nilly. I didn't *want* it to happen. You mentioned earlier that I was influenced by Edward Thomas; I'd never read Edward Thomas at that time – I was in my thirties – and my hero was the urban, wristy Louis MacNeice. I'd already written poems by that time but, as soon as I got to the country, exactly what I thought would happen did happen: I was overtaken by it because it seemed to me *permanent*. I mean, a leaf is permanent: it falls off and it grows, but it seemed to me to relate to creation in a way that life in a town doesn't. I was excited by it. I didn't choose to be excited, I just was.

There's a sort of paradox here. On the one hand, you're deeply pre-occupied with the permanent. You have this word 'presences' which you use in one or two poems and which gave you the title for your New and Selected Poems. *But on the other hand, as you've said, you're dismayed by how autobiographical you are – and that is something temporary, one might think. Why is it that those two things come together in you?*

Well, I think the question can only be answered obliquely. It seems to me, for example, that from the very beginning, we have always felt we were in touch with…let's call it Creation. I mean, Homer: Odysseus would be lost without 'grey-eyed Athene'. He invokes her and he sacrifices to her and she comes and helps him. In other words, a sense of two worlds: of us living simultaneously, not just in this world, but in another too. Men, in various cultures, have evolved systems of gods – and then the Christian system of angels and saints and, in other words, *presences*. This we lost. We lost the language for the expression of it – oh, I don't know when: say Matthew Arnold's 'Dover Beach'. It is now completely gone and yet I feel – I don't know how much I'm like other people, I would suggest I was very normal in this respect – I feel that there is another world and we have a connection with it. I'm as likely to write nonsense about it as anybody else, but I have this intimation of a language that is just out of earshot. We seem to be being told something frequently which we just can't quite hear. If one is to express it honestly, one has to express one's own hesitations about its reality as well. And yet if one believes it and gives faith to it, then, as I said, the only way to share what one feels to be the authenticity of this connection is to place oneself, is to lay oneself on the line – mention who one is, what has happened where one is, the sky, the tree, whatever.

Can we take the point a bit further and say what this adds up to is that you are in some sense a religious poet? And you're a religious poet in a rather unusual sense for modern times in that you talk a great deal about heaven and angels, in other words about the supernatural, the other world. Do you feel yourself to be unusual in that respect, or do you feel that poetry always leads along that path?

I find it very difficult to imagine any poet who has not got some religious dimension. There may be such...I mean, after all, what is a poem? It's an attempt to find the music in the words describing an intuition. (I mustn't, on the hoof, try to define poetry – people have been trying to do that for a very long time.) I would have thought the religious dimension did enter into poetry automatically. Nowadays, of course, it is a question of language. I think one can safely – just about safely, it depends on the context – use a machinery of angels and the heavens. I think those words are still acceptable within a poem, whereas other forms of Christian expression would be either confusing or off-putting.

There's a fairly early poem of yours, a satire for Patrick Creagh, in which you recreate the old notion of the countryside as a retreat. You make an analogy with Sir Thomas Wyatt, and perhaps one also thinks of Andrew Marvell's 'The Garden' and poems of that sort. Is that partly what you see yourself as being – as being in retreat from the world that most people live in today, a world of urban problems and so on?

I think it would be appalling if that were so, and it very possibly is, but at the same time one has to trust one's temperament and one's fate and one's own fortune, good or ill. Knowing myself, I need a very long time to think. I don't thrive on excitement and distraction as some people do, and therefore I would have had to live out of the town I think...because I do get very excited in towns. I mean, wasn't it Rochester who used to say that he was fine until he crossed the Thames, going to London, and then he became like a madman? I'm rather like that. That particular poem, 'Satire I', is based on the metre and form of Wyatt's 'Satire I', in which he is saying more or less the same thing: he's moved away from court in order to think. I was at that time – it was in the Sixties – very much involved with the television satire boom. Oh, my picture was in the papers and I was earning a lot of money and I knew everybody and so on. It seemed to me a contemporary equivalent of the court and I knew that I had to get away from it – for my own sake.

I've seen you described once or twice as somebody who struggles to be an optimist in the teeth of the evidence. Is that correct?

Well, I would have thought it was. It would be appalling to be or to seem complacent, and yet I do feel very strongly that it is part of our duty to *praise*, and there is a technical difficulty there, because if you praise outside a specifically religious context – and we don't have a specifically religious context, in literature anyway – you run the risk of the reader saying: 'Well, it's all right for some!' So you have to include – and it's quite easy to do so – you have to signal your own knowledge that it is not all right for some, nor perhaps is it even all right for yourself. But you certainly must not complain. You must affirm and praise and signal at the same time your knowledge that all is not well.

I mentioned Edward Thomas and Ivor Gurney earlier on. I suppose the analogy is interesting because, although both of them are writers who concentrate on the things of the countryside, of rural life, there are (so to speak) 'noises off' all the time. I feel that in your poetry too: that the countryside is a place from which one gets perspective.

Oh, very much so and, as I said, there's the absence of distraction. Of course, there's nothing one has without paying for it and, as a consequence, one can be thought of as being a sort of marginal ruralist. One can get out of touch with one's friends. All these are prices one has to pay.

Let's talk a little more about Gurney in particular, because you obviously feel some affinity with him. How did you first come across his work?

Well, that's quite interesting because I wonder if it isn't poets who really help other poets to survive. I was first told about him by Geoffrey Grigson. I knew something about him: I knew he'd shared a piano teacher with Ivor Novello and somehow the two things came together, so I thought he was a sort of night-club pianist! Grigson had been told about Gurney by W.H. Auden. 'You must read Gurney,' said Auden to Grigson and Grigson said to me, 'You must read Gurney.' When I did read him it took some time for me to see the point of him, because he is so queer and awkward. And then I came across a poem of his called 'The Silent One', about disobeying an order in the trenches, and I thought: This is just like nothing I've ever read. So I read on. The poem almost had a MacGonagall awkwardness but it worked, and I thought: Is this just luck? Then I realised that he'd had this luck so often that he was obviously a very good poet. I put on a programme about him at the Cheltenham Festival with Geoffrey Grigson and with a singer singing his songs, because of course Gurney was better known as a musician than as a poet. That was advertised in the paper and a man rang up from Gloucester and said would I come along because up in the attic of his sister-in-law, Mrs Gurney, were whole boxes of manuscripts. I went along and I was given them on condition I gave them to the archives. They stayed in my house for a long time and then I was asked to do the edition and I discovered that in these notebooks were masses of excellent poems which had never even been typed, never seen the light of day. People use the word too often, but it actually was a privilege to be handling new, unpublished stuff by Gurney.

Do you think you've learnt from him?

Yes, I think so. Earlier I mentioned Louis MacNeice. One of the most exciting things to me in a poem is the use of a sentence, the way a sentence can spill over the line and perhaps even for two or three lines, and still remain within a form, not a tight form but a recognisable form of verse, usually (in MacNeice's case and in Gurney's case) rhymed verse. I find that brilliantly exciting and Gurney does it a lot. But within that form, there's very little sense of constriction. I feel that both MacNeice and Gurney – two very different kinds of poet – can get the whole of their reality into it. This is a wonderful gift and it's something that I had been trying to do long before I came across Gurney. To some extent therefore he confirmed and encouraged me in my own practice. I also liked the risks he ran, verbally and in all sorts of other ways.

Do you mean things like the ridiculous rhymes?

Oh yes. I come back to the word 'authentic'. He seems to be always authentic in this.

The movement of certain of your lines has a kind of irregularity which is maybe a little reminiscent of him. You write in the standard metres on the whole, but you vary them in ways not quite like anyone else. How do you go about shaping a poem?

Well, the best way I can directly answer your question is to say that I've recently finished a 100-line poem, which for me is a long poem. I only finished it the other day. It's called 'Severn *aisling*'. And I just happen to remember the inspiration of it, which was a walk up the Severn. When I started to write about it, a line came into my head:

'Walking up from your loss, your estuary'. I very much wanted to get away from the pentameter and I realised that had four beats. That pleased me. I then realised that what I was going to write about was really a form of allegory. I had the word 'estuary' and I had the word 'allegory'. I wrote a verse and realised that the lines had to be four beats and that each verse of six lines began with 'estuary' – an 'ee' sound – for the rhyme-word and ended with an 'ee' – 'allegory'. So I felt the form was imposed on me and then the thoughts of the poem or the descriptions of the poem had to be imposed inside that discipline. That's the most recent memory I have of composing.

Is this long poem typical of the work that you're doing now?

No, those are the lucky moments. Some poems just sort of come. They do seem to write themselves and rhyme themselves. (That sounds immensely pretentious but it has been my experience.) I discover that they're rhymed after I've written them. I think I'm going to change my method of writing actually, partly because of this experience, here. I'm much more interested in people than it appears in my poems and I think I'm going to consciously set myself to write some poems about people.

London, 26 November 1990
(Broadcast: 2 December 1990)

John Heath-Stubbs

John Heath-Stubbs has sometimes been called a learned poet. I suspect that this annoys him. Certainly his work is full of recondite knowledge, but there is nothing academic about it, nor does it 'smell of the lamp'. On the contrary, he is arguably the most entertaining poet we have among us, profound and disturbing at times but also extremely funny. As is sometimes the case with learned poets – Milton is the obvious paradigm – he is unconsciously a teacher, and we learn from him in the most painless of ways.

He has something else in common with Milton. For the past 30 years or so, he has been effectively blind. Inescapably, *memory* has played a major role in his later development – in two ways. First, the poems quite plainly draw on remembered knowledge. And secondly, they have taken on something of the character of ancient poetry, composed as they are for the voice more than the page.

His first book was published in 1942. Over the more than 50 years since then, he has published extensively as poet, critic, anthologist and translator. Among his most important books are the epic poem *Artorius* (1972) and, published for his seventieth birthday in 1988, a massive *Collected Poems*. His most recent book, published subsequently to this recording, is *Sweetapple Earth* (1993).

Has the fact that you went totally blind in the 1970s affected the development of your poetry since then?

Well, I think it gave me a new lease of life ultimately because I was much more relaxed, I was no longer fighting a losing battle. I compose on a tape-recorder and you can correct on a tape-recorder just as effectively as when writing it down. I never composed on the typewriter because I think that the inorganic rhythm of the typewriter interferes with the organic rhythm of poetry. I used to compose with a pen on a large piece of double foolscap, so the corrections could be written in on the opposite page. It's much easier in many ways writing on a tape recorder, but I can't type any longer, so I have to find somebody to type it out for me.

You've divided the bulk of your Collected Poems *into two halves which split at around 1965. You print the later half first and the earlier half second. Can you say why you've done this?*

Well, many of the earlier poems have many faults of immaturity and they belong to a period now slightly outmoded. After all, I began to write in the 1940s: this is a decade which, since the Movement and all that, has been often (I think wrongly) decried. I simply felt that, if I printed the earlier poems first, it might have an adverse effect on reviewers, who would start reading the book from the front and only judge me on the earlier poems. I think my later poems are better. So I prefer the later poems to be given more prominence and then people can go and look at the earlier ones and say, 'Well, perhaps these are not so bad after all', which was my own feeling.

The 1940s have been described as a Neo-Romantic period. Is that a term you react to at all?

I wasn't happy with it at the time really because, in many ways, I had always admired the Augustans like Pope and Dryden at least as much as the Romantics. But it was a sort of bandwagon that I rather reluctantly found myself co-opted on to. These terms Romantic and Classic: one used to worry about them a lot when one was an undergraduate. I'm inclined to think they're only terms of taxonomy and they're probably best used simply in a periodic way. Romantic poetry is that written in England between 1798 and, well, 1837 or 1910. Augustan poetry is that written between 1660-something and 1800.

The later part of the period you've called Romantic – I mean, 1837-1910 – is something I wanted to ask you about. Some years ago you wrote a book about what you call 'the later fortunes of Romanticism'.

Yes. You see, I had read English at Oxford during a period when the English School was heavily influenced by the views of C.S. Lewis. He did not believe that you should really study anything academically until it was a hundred years old. He thought this in the 1930s and in the 1940s we were still stopping at 1830-something. Now they go on right to the present day. I think there's something in the Lewis view, but, having taken my degree in English, I really began to study the

Victorians in depth almost for the first time, because I hadn't studied them academically. Also, it was partly to carry on a kind of legacy that had been entailed on me by Sidney Keyes, who was my close friend. He was very interested in the poets who come just between the period of Keats and the period of Tennyson: in Beddoes and Darley and Clare, who were really only discovered in the twentieth century. He said that somebody ought to write a book on them and my first chapter *was* about them. It was after his death; I was almost carrying on a trust. Then I extended the book to cover other poets that might fit in with such a view of nineteenth-century poetry.

Do you feel, though, that you have some kind of affinity with poets like Tennyson and possibly with earlier writers like Beddoes?

Well, I did then. Of course there are many different Tennysons but, as for Beddoes, this was a poet who was re-discovered really in the 1930s – partly because I think he was looked upon as a kind of proto-surrealist, which is one way of looking at him. I think all young men are interested in and fascinated by psychoanalytical and psychological theories because they have all sorts of problems and they hope that, by reading Freud or Jung, they may be able to understand themselves and their problems better. Actually, in the 1940s the influence of Freud was giving way to that of Jung and this interested me in Beddoes. I still admire Beddoes but I'm not fascinated by him now in the way I was then.

Do either of those writers I've mentioned come up in any of your poems as influences?

It's very difficult to know who has influenced you. I've sometimes had students who have been writing dissertations or theses on my work. They come to see me and the first question they ask is: 'Who are your influences?' I say: 'You're supposed to tell me!'

When you came to write your epic poem, Artorius, *you must have had that period to some extent in your mind, if only negatively.*

Not negatively. I'd always been fascinated by that subject. I had been planning an Arthurian poem ever since my undergraduate days. It was partly triggered off by Robert Graves's *Count Belisarius*, which is about a Roman general in the time of Justinian, when the Byzantine Empire temporarily re-conquered Italy. In his preface to that novel, which I think is one of Graves's best historical novels, he says that, if King Arthur had been chronicled by a historian (as Belisarius was by Procopius) instead of by poets and minstrels, we might have a very different picture of a general trying to defend the last remnants of Roman civilisation in England in the sixth century. This idea clicked. It was beginning to be commonplace, in the 1930s and 1940s, that we were perhaps living in a period when civilisation was under threat, in a period not unanalogous to the last days of the Roman Empire. I still think there's some truth in that. At the same time, I have a partly Celtic background. My father's family had Welsh connections and my father was partly brought up in Wales. I never visited Wales as a child, though I did visit Brittany at an early age. And I remember my father talking to me then – I was the age of four – about this being one of the places where King Arthur was. It caught my imagination.

When I said 'negatively' earlier, I was thinking of the fact that your poem is very unlike a Victorian *account of King Arthur.*

Well, of course, it has to be. But there has been a large number of poets, and even more novelists, who have written about King Arthur in recent years, and they really fall into two groups: the Malorians, who like to imagine Arthur in an idealised medieval world, as Tennyson does and as Malory did, and those who have gone to Geoffrey of Monmouth's chronicle and the earlier Welsh sources, who like to see him as a historical figure of the Dark Ages. I read Geoffrey of Monmouth's *History of the Kings of Britain* at school. It was in the school library, and I read it with fascination. It remained vividly in my memory. I read it when I was about thirteen, I think.

One of the things about Artorius *which seems to me to run all through your work, and which perhaps links up with what you were saying about a new Dark Age, is the preoccupation with time and with history – with a sense of time not as consecutive but as in some sense cyclic.*

Yes, I was influenced here by Joyce, by *Finnegan's Wake.* One of the problems about writing a long poem for the twentieth-century poet is, I think, that it mustn't be a novel in verse, because novelists can obviously do that better. It has got to be structured in some way as not to be a direct narrative from A to B. I deliberately planned a cyclic structure to avoid this and used a framework based on a number of recurrent symbols. One of these was the twelve Signs of the Zodiac. Another was the nine Muses, so that each section of the poem was in a different poetic form, or in some cases prose forms, according as to which Muse was presiding at this point.

I suppose the other symbol that one would want to think about here, which particularly occurs in your later poetry, is that of music.

My mother was a professional musician and I had a very strong musical background. I learnt the cello as a boy, but it wasn't my main interest and I gave it up when I went to university. It was really wished upon me by my mother, who had a very strong personality. But at least there was always music in our house and the fact that I studied it, and studied harmony to some extent, gives me perhaps an added appreciation of it. Music is for me perhaps the supreme art because it lies beyond words and beyond images. You cannot say what a piece of music means. I like the story about Beethoven: somebody is supposed to have said, 'What did you mean by that sonata?' And he said, 'This is what I meant,' and played it again.

There's a poem of yours which I think is quite wonderful, the 'Homage to J.S. Bach', which ends with the words 'the great waves of his Sanctus *lifted / The blind art of music into a blinding vision'. That makes me think at the moment of two things. One is obviously the fact that you are yourself blind.*

Yes.

But secondly, that music in that sense seems to belong to the eternal sphere as against the historical one.

Oh I do feel this very strongly of Bach. I take seriously what everybody assumed in the Renaissance, that to some extent music does actualise the transcendent. In the case of Bach, he was partly blind himself in his later years. He was operated on for cataracts, which must have been jolly dodgy in the eighteenth century. Hearing Bach's *B Minor Mass* for the first time, when I was about nineteen or twenty I think, was a tremendous experience for me. I had become in my adolescence totally unbelieving and this was a turning-point because I could not believe that this man was writing this great music about a purely subjective fancy: it must be about something that actually existed. I started the poem about Bach with the idea of writing a tribute to my old harmony master. I remember his once saying to me – I was only about fifteen at the time I think – 'What do you think of Bach?' and I gave some rather foolish, muddled-up, adolescent answer of approval. And this very boring old man, suddenly his eyes shone and he said, 'I think he's the greatest man who ever lived.' But somehow, in the course of composing the poem, he got lost, left out, and there was just Bach!

Music is notable for being orderly in some sense, isn't it?

Yes.

And order is another preoccupation of yours. I wonder if we can talk about just one aspect of it? Taxonomy comes up in your poems a lot, particularly with regard to Natural History.

Yes, I was fascinated by Natural History when I was a boy. I was brought up in the country – educated on the Isle of Wight and brought up in Hampshire. Not exactly in a rural community, but in a residential conurbation where access to fields and woods was very easy, and I wandered about observing birds and flowers and insects and things like that. Also, I was quite fascinated by this idea that they were related and that these relationships could be tabulated in terms of orders and families and precisely in terms of their Latin nomenclature, which I think most people find very dull. Of course, this was in fact a real affinity because what the taxonomists were expressing was the Darwinian idea of descent. This absolutely possessed me. I only began to be able to include this passion of my boyhood in my poetry quite late, but then I did. In fact, I've juist completed another poem about botanical families, which hasn't been published yet.

You have a poem, which I'm very keen on and I suspect you are as well, called 'Plato and the Waters of the Flood'.

Yes, I am very keen on that. This came to me very spontaneously one morning. I had been reading a book on Orphism by a scholar called Guthrie. Orphism was an ancient Greek mystery religion supposed to have been founded by Orpheus and Guthrie told this curious story about there being a fountain in the centre of Asia Minor which the Turks called Plato's Spring, because that's where Plato brought the waters of the Flood to an end by making them flow backwards underground. His idea was that there may have been a historical Orpheus, a religious prophet, but he would bear about as much relationship to the Orpheus we all know about as the real Plato to this legendary one. But a week or so later, early one morning, I got up and took a walk in the park and it somehow gelled as a symbol: Plato controlling the flood as a symbol of the attempt by the abstract intellect to control the formless. But the formless is also the creative and we know that Plato had to expel the poets from his ideal Republic.

One of the reasons I asked you about it was because – paradoxically, in view of what we've been saying – in that poem the poets seem to take the side of chaos against order.

Yes, exactly. That's why Plato expelled them: because he said poetry was lies. They told lies about the gods. They should have been writing moral propaganda. So, in a certain sense, poets *are* on the side of disorder.

But they're also on the side of order, are they not?

Yes, this is a paradox, yes – which I felt and feel very strongly in myself. That is why I think this poem gelled in the way it did.

Do you think that that paradox is the root of all poetry in some sense?

Yes, it may well be. Keats, you remember, talks about the necessity for the poet being in 'doubts and difficulties and uncertainties'.

The Negative Capability.

Yes, it's in the same passage about the Negative Capability. I think, in this world, this is what poetry has got to be about. As soon as it becomes totally committed to an ideology, it probably dies.

London, 14 December 1990
(Broadcast: 7 January 1991)

Tony Harrison

At the heart of Tony Harrison's recent play, *The Trackers of Oxyrhynchus*, is his version of a fragmentary satyr play by Sophocles. But in Harrison's adaptation the Chorus of Satyrs – still goat-like and phallic, to be sure – is transformed into a squad of beery, North-Country clog-dancers. It is perhaps an attempt at resolving the conflict at the core of Harrison's work – between his polyglot erudition and his roots in working-class Leeds, between classical culture and class culture. Harrison has degrees in Classics and Linguistics, has travelled all over the world and is conversant with several modern languages, including Hausa and Czech. Yet the more he travels in his art, the more insistently he returns to his home territory, where he finds himself cut off from his class, his family and – most ironically – the language he grew up with.

Harrison's adaptations for the stage of Molière, Racine, Aeschylus and the medieval Mysteries represent a one-man renaissance of verse-drama in English. At the same time he remains a formidable lyric poet, though increasingly one who takes on the big public themes of the day: the miner's strike of 1984, the Salman Rushdie affair and, in his most recent book *The Gaze of the Gorgon* (1992), the Gulf War.

I've heard it said that when you were quite young, you made a resolution to earn your living from writing poetry. Is that true?

I don't actually remember a date where I made a specific resolution, but I certainly had a kind of grim determination that I would like the whole venture of my life to be poetry – including earning my living.

You've scored another success recently in the theatre with The Trackers. *It seems to many of us that with your dramatic works you've managed to do something which for a long time was thought*

*impossible – which is to write verse-drama for the modern stage.
How do you think it is that you've succeeded in that where others
have failed?*

I think it is by taking a circuitous route through translating and
adapting some of the plays written when verse was extremely ambitious dramatically. When I was wanting to write plays as a very young
man, I moved on to a world of theatre which I felt had been anaes-
thetised and genteelised by Eliot and Fry; that it had really become
drawing-room plays versified rather than finding a real *use* for verse.
It seems to me that in the great periods of theatre, the ones that draw
me – whether it's the Greeks or Shakespeare and the Jacobeans or
Molière or Racine or Goethe – the poets always worked directly with
actors and found a style which, rather than concealing the fact that
it's verse, drew attention to the physicality of its mechanics. I was
very drawn to that, not only from my studies, but also from traditional pantomime – which was my first experience of theatre – which
was in verse and which in fact includes many of the things I like to
include in the theatre I do: men playing women, women playing men,
verse, transformations...

So in a sense one of the things that happens in The Trackers *specifically happens in all your plays, in that you introduce something of
what is normally thought of as 'low art' into 'high art'...*

Oh yes, I think that I've taken very strong impressions from popular
theatre that I had as a child and often used them to unlock classical
plays. In fact I remember having a dream when we were casting for
The Oresteia, which I did with Peter Hall at the National Theatre. I
had a dream in which a lot of old men came to sign a book I had by
the door, wanting to be in the Chorus for *The Oresteia* (which begins
with a chorus of old men), and in the morning I read the book and all
the names were Norman Evans, Nat Jackley, etc. – all the people I'd
seen in the pantomime as a child – and that gave me a kind of clue to
the always audience-directed intention of popular theatre. The difference between that theatre and verse theatre that I found as an
aspiring verse-dramatist is enormous.

*It might be thought that that was not possible with drama like
Racine's or even Molière's, which is thought to be rather frigidly
classical, but in those cases you found devices for making them more
relevant to modern conditions – like making* The Misanthrope *happen in 1966 rather than 1666. Do you think you always have some
notion of relevance behind what you do?*

If it's a question of re-theatricalising a classic from a previous period, then you often use a tactic like that as much to allow the kind of language you can feel creative in as simply to change the costumes.

Some of the plays we've been talking about – for instance, The Trackers *– share obvious themes with the poems – themes about class, for instance, themes about division of one sort or another. It struck me looking again at your* Selected Poems *that those weren't exactly the themes at the outset. I mean, with* The Loiners *the most obvious theme was sexual life of one sort or another and I wondered if you came to think that that was really the same theme as the one you've made your name with, which is the class theme?*

After the publication of *The Loiners*, I remember my mother being offended by the book – by its sex, its outspokenness about sexual activity; also that a great many of the poems were not understood by my parents, and by people like my parents, and I began to wonder what was this enormous effort to acquire what I call *eloquence*, which was through long commitment to becoming a poet, but also an obsessive commitment to all forms of articulation, language-learning and so on. I think the shock of that reaction made me think: Well, for what purpose is this eloquence being acquired if it has no direct access to the people I grew up amongst and whom I love?

And did that then lead you on to what you might call a political theme – I mean in the broad sense of politics?

I think it's that both in a narrow sense and also in a broader sense. Many of the poems dramatise the divisions which are later dramatised in *Trackers*. That is, between having what, being a reader, you could call a literary or poetic experience and a device or a technique I think I've developed of suddenly looking over my own shoulder. Or, to take an image from cinematography, of suddenly moving the camera back and showing the reader either in a sort of privileged isolation or in relation to those things which do not seem accessible or convertible or metamorphosable into poetry. I've always wanted to know what is left out when you make certain choices to create a style.

Can you give an example of that perhaps?

Well – it's like Baudelaire saying 'Hypocrite lecteur' – saying you've got to the point of being gratified with literary experiences or theatrical experiences but let us now pay our dues – let us pay the cost of that privilege of literacy by using our sharpened senses to look beyond the poem or the play in which we are momentarily contained.

Is that partly why, for instance, a lot of the sonnets in 'The School of Eloquence' – your sequence of sixteen-line sonnets – contain quotations from non-literary persons?

Yes, it's a deliberate contrast to the kind of poetry which bolstered itself up with quotations from many other cultural sources – like other languages, whether they were Latin, Greek or Sanskrit.

Like Pound and Eliot?

Like Pound and Eliot. In a way I was educated in that tradition but then I seemed to want to set – rather than a jewel from past literature – a found iambic pentameter in the speech of the working class for example. So that often they're very deliberately non-literary sources which actually could be taken absolutely untouched from speech. I often quote examples of hearing perfect iambic pentameters all around me. If your ear is tuned to it, you hear them. I always remember the one I've often quoted – the woman I heard on the train explaining to a stranger where her son-in-law worked and she said, 'He works for British Gypsum outside Leek' – which is a perfect iambic pentameter. And then she made one that was rather more adventurous like 'Well, it's the whole world over, the unrest'. I enjoy finding things which will fit the metre – like the first poem in 'The School of Eloquence', which will always be the first poem, 'On Not Being Milton'. That ends with a quotation from a condemned Cato Street conspirator: 'Sir, I Ham a very Bad Hand at Righting' – which is metrically sound in that context, but which comes from a source whose speech normally disappears with them, which is never recorded in the rolls of honour or by historical scribes or in any other form – except in a moment like this when he was about to be executed. Therefore death had given a weightier significance to his language.

A kind of Shakespearean unconscious tragic grandeur.

Yes.

It seems to me that there's a sort of irony behind this: that in that sequence, 'The School of Eloquence', you talk about the ownership of language by a class. And you also talk in one of the poems about losing your mother-tongue, meaning in a sense the tongue that you learnt with your mother. But it also seems that, by these means you've been talking of, in a sense you've regained your mother-tongue, you've regained ownership of what was lost. Do you feel that?

Yes, it's like taking an odyssey and returning and finding what you're looking for at the place you left. I feel that very strongly. So when you're first exposed to the kind of education that we were exposed to...I have a poem describing how I wasn't allowed to read poetry...

'Them & [uz]'.

'Them & [uz]'. And in fact that retrospective aggro has been a source of a lot of my theatrical activity – reclaiming Northern classics like *The Mysteries*, using Northern inflections in *The Oresteia*, for example, and in the most recent work, *The Trackers of Oxyrhynchus*. But the speech I had was considered ugly by comparison with RP or Queen's English or whatever the standard form was, which we know is based on the speech of the Southern public school, and there was a process of dubbing which I found very bewildering – and it works in the theatre in some ways still – that you learn a certain way of speaking Shakespeare or other classical plays. There's no reason for this except cultural and political reasons.

This reminds me particularly now of a more recent work, the poem 'v', where you have a little dialogue between yourself and an imaginary skinhead who's defaced your parents' grave and who then turns out to be a kind of alter ego. I wonder how strongly you sympathise and identify with that skinhead. For instance, there was a kind of scandal surrounding the poem because you read it on television and it was mentioned in Parliament and so on, and it did actually occasion your using four-letter words in the nation's sitting rooms. I wonder how much you chose to do that, wanted to do that, or how much you were unconsciously relishing the opportunity?

Everything about 'v' was deliberately public and public certainly means – in our terms – television, so that I was very glad that it was on television. That's the kind of audience I feel poetry should have. I certainly didn't put in four-letter words in order to make a scandal – they were an essential part of the poem; it's a poem which ranges from the graveyard's use of Latin for epitaphs down to the 'fuck' and the 'shit' that are inscribed on the graves. And these are examples of modes of language – both of which have their own kinds of power and the poem really is about power and the power over language.

But I mean there is a sense in which, by – as a poet – taking on the four-letter words, you give that skinhead a kind of power which he actually didn't have before...

But he has a certain kind of power when someone like me sees the grave of his loved ones defaced. I mean, that is a powerful act and it comes from some need and my wanting to understand that need is what created the poem. And also thinking about where I should be buried for example. Then you realise that the graveyards of the past, which were centres for fairly stable communities who assumed generations would stay in the same place, are no longer so, and that everywhere in Britain you could duplicate the graveyard that I wrote about. I had many letters from people saying exactly that – several graveyards in several cities were equally defaced.

Of course, this brings us to another side – almost the opposite side of your poetry – which is that in some ways it's very traditional. That poem is obviously based on Gray's 'Elegy in a Country Church-yard'....

True…

…and in all sorts of ways your poems invoke what has been done in the art in the past – as indeed lots of other people's poems do – but it comes across as rather striking in your case, because you seem to be so consciously speaking for the dispossessed and inarticulate and yet making them speak in effect through these ancient forms, metres, conventions, etc. Do you ever find that a contradiction, or is it to you a seamless construction?

No, it's a deliberately dramatised contradiction. It's a way both of testing the aspiration towards eloquence – of giving it a place in which to be heard – but also a way of subjecting the classical form, which I think still has its meaning, to those things which you would think most likely to destroy it. Like putting a beautiful object in a wind tunnel to test its stress. So the two things happen at the same time: there's a reclamation, re-energising of the classical form to the point when it might begin to crumble and, by doing that, you also give voice to an aspiration or a motivation that would not normally seek a poetic place to be heard.

In doing that, do you think that you in some sense salvage the classi-cal, as well as speaking for the dispossessed?

Yes, there is a recycling process, a reclamation deliberately going on there. There are many things being dramatised, many ways of look-ing at the same form, the same art that has had a life of many gener-ations, many centuries – how can it be reclaimed, how can it be rescued from simply being the kind of art which creates a closed order of appreciators, for example. This is what *The Trackers of*

Oxyrhynchus dramatises. You're in a desert in which there are two Oxford archaeologists who are reclaiming – trying to rediscover – fragments of a spiritual past with workmen who look at the fragile papyri – because it's in a desert and it's the only organic matter around – as fertiliser. So the idea of fertiliser is there in both senses. And at another level – and one of the deepest levels of the poetry – it's what is the difference between material need and spiritual need, or between cultural need and material need.

You talk in your introduction to The Trackers *of Greek drama as 'open-eyed about suffering but with a heart still open to celebration and physical affirmation'. Is it the case that you're drawn to ancient drama because you see in it an opportunity for healing – if only for a time – the sorts of division and conflict we've been talking about?*

Yes, I think I'm drawn to Greek drama for many reasons and one of the reasons why I didn't want to let oblivion totally reclaim the satyr play was that that seemed to be one of the clues to how the Greeks maintained a kind of celebratory route in the sensual and everyday to follow their tragedy. What I have used it to look for is a style with which we might be able to confront *our* worst: just as when I take the most traditionally literate form and subject it to an illiterate attack and see if it sustains it, so do I think that our need for celebration has to admit and openly acknowledge the huge darkness of the twentieth century, in which it seems that simple spirit of affirmation has been burnt out.

So, behind all the darkness of the poetry, there's a kind of hope present all the time?

The poem itself is that act – I think the poem itself is that act of affirmation.

London, 14 January 1991
(Broadcast: 4 February 1991)

Les Murray

Until quite recently, no English-speaking poet from outside the British Isles or the United States could hope for much of a reputation in Britain. The few who achieved one did so by coming to live here. This lack of interest had little to do with the quality of the poetry, particularly in the case of Australia, a country which has produced many remarkable poets: Judith Wright, A.D. Hope, James McAuley – the list is a long one. The surprising range of Australian poetry was recently documented in *The New Oxford Book of Australian Verse*, which takes the reader far back into the nineteenth century and – where Aboriginal verse is concerned – probably beyond.

The New Oxford Book was edited by Les Murray, who is effectively the first Australian poet to have broken through the barriers of indifference. He was born in rural New South Wales in 1938, the only child of a poor farming family. He has recently proclaimed his loyalty to his roots by settling on a farm in his home region. But he continues to write prolifically: a weighty *Collected Poems* appeared in 1992 and his eleventh slim volume, *Translations from the Natural World*, in 1993. His manner unites the down-to-earth egalitarianism of the new world with an almost mystical feeling for the quiddity of things. Characteristically, he dedicates all his books 'To the Glory of God'.

I know you grew up on a dairy farm in New South Wales. But it's hard, I think, for an English person to imagine quite what life was like in that part of the world at that time. Can you give us some idea?

It was a remote life: we were sort of outside of Western civilisation to a degree. We saw the newspapers and there was a bit of radio around, although not many people had it. We told each other stories – we went in for scandal and gossip, and all-night dances and sing-songs, and this kind of thing. It was fairly self-contained kind of culture, which in many ways had come almost unchanged from Scotland. That melted away to a large degree in my lifetime. The place is much more cosmopolitan and open to everything now: the television has got in and the post office has gone away – there's no longer a place where you meet, you talk to each other on the phone – and it's different. But it's not all gone. I made the distinction the other day that in the old days we used to sit around the fire to tell each other stories; now we tell them standing up! At work!

Was that atmosphere, do you think, conducive to poetry?

Oh yes. It was full of the wild poetry of malice and gossip and wit and that sort of thing – nicknaming and casual little remarks: some of my father's one-liners have ended up in my poems – they're wonderful. Formal poetry as such, though, was represented mostly by Australian bush balladry which was recited by men when half-drunk and, when they were fully drunk, they recited Bobby Burns. I didn't see much poetry and it wasn't taught in schools very much and certainly Australian poetry was barely mentioned in schools.

When did you first get to know formal poetry?

Towards the end of high school. I started to be fascinated by Gerard Manley Hopkins first, and I was led to poetry by a couple of good English teachers and by the sports master, who happened to know about Australian poetry. I didn't know it existed – it wasn't taught in schools – and I began to read Kenneth Slessor and Judith Wright and Doug Stewart and many other people and I said to myself: I can do this. I was wanting to make art of some sort. I couldn't paint very much and I had no ear for music. I'd tried to write a novel and I found I wasn't much interested in the story – it was a ridiculous story anyway. But when I found poetry, this was an art of encapsulations and captures and presence; and the things that I was interested in – like the knocking of stones together in a stream, or the sound of the wind in the trees – were just as important as the humans in a poem, and I thought: Yes, that's it – that's the whole world, you know, it's not just the human world.

So you started from the sensuous things?

Sure, and I've stuck there I think. I'm more interested in presence than anything else perhaps. You know: make it present.

From the point of view of language – do you think you were born at a lucky time? I'm thinking of how Australia has entered a kind of post-colonial phase now...

Yes, I was born at a lucky time. There were very fine poets who were born too early. England was still in her aristocratic dream at that time – her Empire dream – and everybody had their allotted roles and one of ours was not to be cultured. And you used to get this old one of 'One doesn't associate Australia with culture.' That ended the day in Cardiff when a fellow asked me on the BBC – he said: 'Erm, Australia, one doesn't associate Australia with culture.' And I said: 'One doesn't associate that remark with culture!' Never been used since! But the time was right for it. In a way, we came into acceptance on the back of the Africans, because they began to be studied – post-colonial literature – and there was no theoretical basis on which we could be kept out and they could be let in. And so to some extent we came up the back stairs that were called Commonwealth Literature Studies in universities and then we got into the publishing world. The publishing machine is so big it needs grist all the time for its mills, and that's part of the reason too.

But you're not very happy, are you, about the association of poetry with the universities?

It's an uncomfortable, scratchy relationship because universities over-explain, I think. I wrote a poem which ends: 'Nothing's free that is explained.' Exegesis is fine, but interpretation can be intrusive and bullying and finally it's police work – unless it's done very sensitively and done with love. Only love can excuse the element of intrusion that's involved. And it'll always try to control poetry down into the status of explanatory prose.

I want to ask you about something which I think is connected with that. You have a poem called 'The Quality of Sprawl' and you celebrate sprawl, expansiveness, bagginess in a way. When I was brought up to read poetry – and I'm sure it must have been the same for you – we were taught that poetry had to be tight, condensed and economical…

It does except when it shouldn't be, you know, except when you want to do something else…

What I was going to ask you about was whether 'sprawl' was in a sense a sort of reaction against tightness?

No, it was just the way that poem should be written and it was that aspect of Australia, of a particular kind of culture which involves sprawl, that wanted celebrating; so I celebrated it! I'm tight when I need the corsets and loose when I need the harem pants sort of thing.

This kind of expansiveness that you go in for is also in a sense a kind of inclusiveness I think ...

Yes, yes, I hate relegation of any sort – I hate people being left out. Of course, that I suppose has been the main drama of my life – coming from the left-out people into the accepted people and being worried about the relegated who are still relegated. I don't want there to be any pockets of relegation left.

You were talking earlier about presence, and I suppose, when I talk about inclusiveness, I'm thinking about the way you celebrate in your poetry the range and variety of the world.

Yes, I love that.

And you say, in a recent epigrammatic poem, 'Poetry is presence.' I wonder if you can just expound what you mean by that phrase?

Well, I think that's what we do essentially. We combine, we fuse together the conscious and the dreaming minds and the body into a whole which is something I call 'wholespeak' – it's a crude term, but it'll serve. People seem to need a measure of that in their lives: they'll get it from poetry, or they'll get it from ideology, they'll get it from their hobbies, or their religion, or somewhere, and nothing is created without it. And I think the effect of it is to make whatever is its subject-matter present and eternal in contemplation. It's as if we've put our hands through a kind of impalpable glass and made something which is beyond death. It's permanently there and it's something we long to join ourselves: we would like eventually to be in the poem ourselves. It's the only way I can figure Heaven to myself actually, that eventually one day you get into the poem and live there.

It's an uncanny feeling to read a poem that has that in it. I think the first one of yours I read was the poem called 'The Burning Truck', where a lorry catches fire and it turns into a kind of divine presence ...

It goes on and on beyond likelihood and possibility. The wild boys in the street follow it. It's not essentially a good noumen, though, that they're following. What I was thinking about when I wrote it was the Nazis – you know, what would I have done in the thirties? If I'd been a kid in Germany in the thirties, might I have followed the parade? If I'd been a kid in Russia at another time, might I have followed the parade and made myself guilty of a lot of things. And the burning truck, I suppose you could say it's heroin, it's Nazis, it's ... significance itself. It's the thing that calls us away from the quotidian world – that's the opposite of presence in a way, although the truck has presence in the poem. It's the opposite of what I'd like to see, which is to give that world so great a presence that no truck could lead you away on a delusive sort of wild-goose chase.

What about myth? Myth is surely connected with this too. You have, for instance, a verse-novel called The Boys who Stole the Funeral, *which is a kind of quest myth, I suppose...*

Yes, it's a Grail legend in a way – but it's a sort of inverse Grail, it's a democratic Grail, it's not the aristocratic Grail which admits only the very pure and the very noble. It's the other one which people can't avoid. They can avoid it, but they're always offered it. It's the Grail of common experience and the common lot and to eat from it, the poem seems to suggest, is wiser and healthier than not to yield. You'll get into a distorted position if you don't. You'll starve for it as well.

This knack that you have of giving the reader presence in that way or turning ordinary experience into myth – I'm tempted to ask you how you do it, but it's troubling in a way because one feels that if you did it consciously you wouldn't get a poem out of it.

No, you can't do all of a poem consciously. That's really the core of my worry with universities – the way that rationalism and the various religions that power universities tend to try and translate all of the world into prose, into rational daylight thinking, and it can't be done. You starve. You starve and then you go mad on that diet. As Goya said, 'The sleep of reason produces monsters.' As I say, 'The waking daylight of reason produces monsters.' The quest has to be through wholeness, because that's how it really works, that's how we structure reality. Something I've always been after – I wasn't conscious of it, I gradually worked out what it was – was something I call 'The Iliad of Peace'. The Western literary tradition starts with Homer, which is a story of war, and then goes on to a wonderful story of adventures and fighting and things until it gets home again. But another start for us might have been with Hesiod, who's talking about the arts of peace and of farming. In some ways Christianity is the Iliad of Peace. It seems that we need that balance. I once wrote in a poem, 'All stories are of war,' so I almost silenced myself out of writing stories from that point on, because they're always about conflict and what I'm after is another thing which I'm calling 'presence' at the moment, which is a basis for peace.

One of the things I notice in your poetry is that you seem to be fundamentally a kind of landscape poet.

Well…

You don't think that?

Yes, sometimes it's a landscape from the inside – describe it from either side, you know…

I have a sense (in the poems) of childhood being associated with particular places and no speech intruding on the places until you write poems about them.

Well, that's probably being an only child. I mean, I didn't talk much till I was nine; there was nobody to talk to – most of my friends were animals. I had no brothers and sisters, and parents were being parents and getting on with their lives, and I listened a lot but I didn't talk much. I only met other children when I was nine – it was probably a bit late. That's part of it, I guess, and also place is terribly important in Australian culture in general. It's utterly important to the oldest Australian culture and a bit of that, I think, seeps in round the edges of everybody's consciousness: a bit of Aboriginal consciousness of place. Of course, places are sacred in Aboriginal stories and you pick up these stories…places that you've been going to all your life, one day you learn the story that was attached to them.

That's like the first poem in your anthology, in fact, the Aboriginal poem…

Yes, Sam Woolagoodja taking his grandchildren up into his country, the Worora country in the Kimberleys, and showing them the caves of the Wandjina paintings – that's it. Life has got these particular centres which are the sacred places of stories, and that's a natural human thing. I think most people anywhere in the world have got certain sacred places which stories revolve around. It's just that the Aborigines made a culture on the basis of it; they wouldn't even farm the land – they didn't want to distort it to hurt the stories. The mystery of Aborigines is why they didn't take up farming – because it existed next door in New Guinea. They obviously saw it, but they seem to have decided against it and I suspect it's because they didn't want to disrupt the fabric of song.

Obviously what we're talking about partly is the intersection of time and place, isn't it? I mean that it's history embodied in place…

Yes, the Aborigines say of a sacred place that it is dream-time there, which is the most succinct description of it I know, and what I'm saying is it's presence there.

A lot of the recent poems in Dog Fox Field *and some of the books just before it have a kind of satirical component, or at any rate a socially critical component…*

Yes, I've been known to bite the odd hand, you know…

Do you enjoy biting hands?

No, it's a thing you mustn't do too much of and I'm going to do less of it. It's not healthy – it makes you ill in the long run if you do it too much, and I've deliberately stepped away from it. I've recently written forty poems called 'Presence: Translations from the Natural World'. One of them mentions a human, but he's a very special human: he's Jesus and it's called 'Animal Nativity' – it's really for the animals around the crib. But all the rest of them are animals, birds, reptiles, molluscs, all sorts of things including even a DNA molecule. I thought I'd get away from the human for a while because I'd been getting a bit sharp and snappish and it's bad for you.

I suppose it's the other side of the coin with regard to your religion, isn't it? I mean, your religiousness necessitates some kind of moral attack on what you see as betrayal of good values…

In the end, though, you run close to that commandment which says 'Judge not lest you be judged', and you'd better not run too close to that one or you'll start destroying yourself – and doing no good to the people you criticise. People really won't take censure. You can make it awfully clear how you see it, but in the end I think you ought to give them something better than a cut over the hand.

Can we say something about form? I'm thinking of The Boys Who Stole The Funeral *again, because that's a poem which, as it were, combines two different sorts of form: it has narrative such as you might find in a novel, but it's also written in versions of the sonnet, so it's like a sonnet sequence.*

That's right, and I couldn't write a damn thing of it until I found a form for it. I started off writing it sort of seriatim down the page and it used to go dead on me within about twenty lines every time; and I finally happened to see a book of sonnets with two sonnets on the left hand page and two on the right and I thought, 'I've got it, I've got my structure.' I could do anything with it because a sonnet has room in it for meditation and for action in the one unit, and all you've got to do with it of course is play endless variations on the sonnet form: turn it upside down, turn it inside out, put the six lines in the middle and the eight lines around them and all this kind of thing. I had great fun with that. One of these days, if I ever write another verse-novel, I've got another form for that too, which I call the 'steps and stairs' method. I won't go into it now and give away the trade secrets. But I've got my form; I just need my story now. Except I'm worried by that thing that I discovered that all stories are of war, and if I could find a story that was not of war, that led away from conflict, I'd be happier.

I'm interested in that form particularly, because it satisfies the requirements of the form but it also in a sense creates a new form.

Yes, well I was trying to recapture for poetry some of the ground we had lost in the eighteenth, particularly nineteenth century, to the novel, which was a very unrespectable form when it first came in. It was regarded as lower than bad soap opera and morally bad for you – but it took over, it took away most of our traditional ground. We were left with the lyric and not much else, and I was trying to capture a bit back.

Do you feel generally about form that you don't like simply to fulfil the traditional requirements but that you like to make something that hasn't been made before out of it?

My fulfilment of traditional requirements always sort of gets drunk as it goes along: I start fulfilling them and then I start playing with them and playing variations on them and leapfrogging over them and it goes like that. I like to find out where a poem goes. If I know the end of a poem before I start, it's probably going to be a dead poem. You throw yourself into it. People used to ask me in school: 'Your poems don't seem to end, Mr Murray, they seem to stop.' And I took a long time to think of the right answer for it and really it's pre-sence all over again. I said: 'Yes, the end is all through the poem. You don't need a clincher on the end which tells you what to think about it. The end is all through it.' And I realised later and used that in the 'Presence' poems. That's one of the definitions of presence – it's the end all through the story.

Because it's infinite?

Yes, try to make little manageable-size vessels on earth which will hold infinity.

*You're part of a new phenomenon, I suppose, which is the poet from
a non-metropolitan region of the world who's acquired an audience
in the metropolis.*

Yes, that metropolitan thing is really a Greek invention. It's an
Athenian thing to do down Boeotia – the old terrible rival thieves.
And the Romans took it up and coarsened it and made it more or less
mandatory that the only centre of civilisation in their empire was
Rome itself – everything had to go there to be validated. Alexandria
held out fairly well against it, but this model became habitual in
Western culture. It disappeared a bit in the Middle Ages – that was
a decentralised culture – but it came in hard again with the Renaissance and we began to concentrate our culture into centres, so that
in the end only about five square miles of the world were regarded as
truly valid cultural centres. They were one square mile in London,
one square mile in Paris, one in New York, etc, and it's all pretty
ridiculous. I reckon the centre of the world is wherever a person is. I
reckon the centre of the world is in fact wherever a living thing is, and
the cultural realisation seems to be spreading at the moment that this
is true – that if you don't say that then you're oppressing most of the
world, you're relegating the Third World. The Third World is in fact
an invention to overcome this precise bad tendency of Western civilisation. The terrible price of metropolitanism is that people *will* go
there. If they think that only that place is the good place, they'll go
there and so, I think, a lot of the reason that the metropolitan idea is
crumbling is the fear of Europeans that everybody else will come to
live in Europe – want to live in the Metropolis. If you tell them
they're civilised where they are, they might stay at home.

How important is Australia itself to you?

Very – and I don't really think I can write about anywhere else
because I don't truly understand the weather and the air and the light
and that sort of thing. I really only understand that of Australia. So
my imagery tends to be Australian – and I tend to think that outside
of our continent I'd probably write tourist verse. I have done it on
occasion, but I think it's probably better done by those who belong
there.

London, 13 March 1991
(Broadcast: 5 May 1991)

Michael Longley

It is often observed that the number of fine poets from Northern Ireland is out of all proportion to the region's size. The achievement is sometimes credited to the Troubles: good poetry – so the argument runs – tends to emerge under pressure. Less often noticed is the fact that few of the poets concerned are political by temperament. It is the strength of Michael Longley's work, for instance, that the political enters it somewhat against the grain. Even in its absence, as in much of his most recent book *Gorse Fires*, it gives an edge to the personal and the particular.

Longley was born in Belfast in 1939 and studied Classics at Trinity College, Dublin. He has been lucky in his friends. In Dublin he got to know Derek Mahon, a fellow-Ulsterman, and the two began discussing each other's poems. Shortly afterwards, back in Belfast, he made friends with Seamus Heaney, whom he met at a now-famous writers' workshop that was run by the poet and critic Philip Hobsbaum. These literary friendships have been a vital ingredient in the growth of Longley's work.

Gorse Fires is his first book for twelve years but, in spite of the long pause, he is a poet of some substance. His *Poems 1963-1983* is quite a bulky collection and maturity is the keynote to *Gorse Fires*: it is fluent and lyrical, yet at the same time economical. You feel he is a poet who has learnt to say only what is essential and who is quite sure of what can be left to inference.

That period in the 1960s when you were working with Seamus Heaney and Derek Mahon: was that a very exciting time for you?

It was very exciting. Derek Mahon and I had become friends at Trinity College, Dublin, in the early 1960s and were already battling with each other and showing off and flexing our muscles. Then I went back to Belfast. Philip Hobsbaum had been running 'The Group' (as it was called) for some time then and the two star-turns were Seamus Heaney and the playwright Stewart Parker. I came in rather late in the day and was immediately dismissed as a kind of campus dandy. My hero in those days was Richard Wilbur. Another was Wallace Stevens, and e.e. cummings. So I consorted rather oddly with the Seamus Heaney who was writing 'Digging' and 'Follower' and all his rather beautiful agricultural poems in the first book. But there was a great sense of competition. What Philip gave us was a sense that we weren't on our own. Belfast in those days was really something of a cultural Siberia. Philip gave us the sense that Belfast might matter and that we mattered and that poetry mattered. It was all done with enormous electrical intensity, these workshops, these discussions. The sheets were cyclostyled beforehand and you had a week or so to read the poems. When your own poems were being dissected, you went there with enormous butterflies in your stomach.

I sometimes think that you are still rather different from Seamus Heaney and that possibly you suffer a little in the comparison from your own particular virtues not being adequately recognised. It seems to me, for instance, that form is a much more important thing for you than for him, that it's a more absolute and final kind of thing.

I think we're both formalists. I've probably in the past carried it to greater extremes than Seamus Heaney. I think it's a very good thing for poetry that its most popular poet is such a good poet. I would hasten to add that I don't write in his shadow and, to be honest with you, that I quite like my position. I mean, if (as you imply) I am underrated, I think it's better to be underrated than overrated. I would hate to be going around thinking I was overrated. As it is, I've had far more success than I ever dreamed of when I was twenty-three or twenty-four, and I regard my friendship with Heaney and with Mahon as a central part of my experience.

Could you talk a little bit about the way you see form? For instance, in your new book, there are very few poems that are rhymed, and yet the poems stand on the page in a very balanced, often symmetrical manner.

I find form one of the mysteries. In my first book, which in many ways is still my favourite book, I think every line rhymes. At that stage I did enjoy taking advantage of all the things that words do: that is to say, arrange themselves in rhythmic patterns and rhyme. Part of the inspiration was in setting myself difficult tasks. I mean, when Yeats was asked where he got his ideas from, he said: 'Looking for the next rhyme'. He wasn't being altogether glib; there is some truth in that. But for some reason, I find it difficult to rhyme now. I'm interested in forms that are, if you like, more organic. I wouldn't want to think that the forms in my earlier books are inorganic but I have now to let the poems happen. There's very little deliberation in what I do. It's the difference between trimming a hedge and building a wall. I think with the earlier poems there's a certain amount of wall-building. I get a rush of feelings and emotions and I reach for the most spontaneous and natural form, but obviously old habits die hard. I write my poems out in long-hand and I think: 'My God. This is going to be a marvellous bit of Frank O'Hara/Raymond Carver free splodge.' Then I go to the typewriter and it's the same old squares-and-oblongs (as Auden says). So I can't help it. It's obviously in my genetic make-up, that poems are for me, still a little too tidy.

You studied Classics as a young man, didn't you? I wonder if that had anything to do with it. I notice for instance in the new book that you have a number of poems which are based on passages from the Odyssey. *There's something very appropriate in this feeling of general formality with absence of rhyme.*

Yes, I enjoyed Classics, although I maintained my amateur status throughout my studies and I regard myself as a lapsed classicist now. I mean, I have very little Latin and Greek, but one of the things the Classics taught me was 'the beauty of things difficult' (or whatever Yeats's phrase was): tracing a long sentence in an Aeschylean chorus, hunting around feverishly for the main verb – that sort of challenge. I think one of the things I picked up from Latin and Greek was syntax: the power of the sentence: how you can release energy by measuring the sentence against the metrical unit and that you can build up enormous pressure if you keep the sentence going on for some time. But that requires a knowledge of syntax.

Can you give an example of that?

Well, in 'Laertes' and in 'Anticlea' I have sustained the sentence from the first word right the way through. I've done it in such a way that I hope nobody will notice that that's what I've done, but that was part of the challenge. The difficult syntax of the poem was a formal substitute for the rhyme-schemes and stanzaic shapes which I used in my earlier work.

Throughout your collected poems there are intermittent love poems – very sensual, often very moving. How central are they to your whole enterprise?

If I was going to be remembered by anything, I would hope it would be by a few love poems. It seems to me the hub of what I do and, if I may pursue the wheel image, out from the hub branch the spokes of other concerns, but they're related to the love poetry: children, landscape, places I love, my friends, and so on. If I'm not writing the occasional love poem, I don't feel that I'm in top gear.

In your second book, An Exploded View, *you begin to talk about public concerns – presumably under the impact of the Troubles. This was in the early 1970s, I think. Was it a deliberate decision that you made or did the political circumstances force themselves upon you?*

Yes, they did force themselves upon me and my friends. The Troubles erupted in 1969 and a cry of 'Where are the War Poets?' went up. I mean: 'We've all these poets in Belfast and not one of them's mentioned the Troubles.' It took time for the raw experience of living through the Troubles to settle to an imaginative depth where they could be dealt with. We were quite self-conscious about avoiding rushing in and hitching a ride on yesterday's headlines and cashing in, as it were, on the suffering of our fellow citizens. So the poems, when they emerged – my poems, Derek Mahon's, Heaney's, Simmons's – emerged after marinading for some time. I think that's only right and proper, because a bad poem is bad enough, but a bad poem about something as big as the Troubles is an impertinence and an offence.

The whole question of how the personal and the private on the one hand relates to the public on the other is a very difficult matter. I think a lot of people don't really understand how it is that an art which can be so personal at one stage can become so public at another. That must have been very important for you throughout your career but particularly in the early Seventies.

Yes, I've chosen in a way to mix the two and to feel my way into public crises by exploring private concerns. The fact that my father was a soldier, for instance, in both World Wars led me to ask the simple question: If he were alive now, what on earth would he make of the Troubles? And that simple question allowed me to write three or four poems, which I like to think are tactful poems. For instance our greengrocer, who happened to be a prosperous Catholic, was shot dead by UVF gunmen and I wrote an elegy for him. But I felt obliged to show it to his widow before I published it and she said that she liked it and was grateful for it. In a sense one has to do the equivalent on a larger scale with anything one writes about the troubles of one's own community.

After the period in which the Troubles featured quite prominently in your poetry, you moved into something of a silence. You haven't published a book in twelve years, and now we have this new collection Gorse Fires. *Was that period of silence painful for you?*

Yes, it was agony really. I thought I was finished. I didn't think I was going to write any more poetry and it was like having an enormous itch which I couldn't scratch. I think most good poetry is written by young people or by old people. I think of the artists who've crowned their careers with marvellous work – like Yeats and Hardy, or in music, Janáček and Verdi. But it's the bloody middle stretch that's difficult. I mean, I was, until very recently, an officer in the Arts Council of Northern Ireland and one's responsibilities are at their optimum round about middle age when one's children are growing up and one's parents and in-laws are getting older. The male menopause. It was an agony. With regard to the Troubles – the new book is, I suppose, relatively speaking more private. But the Troubles and my personal turmoil as a result of not being able to write and as a result of ceasing to enjoy my job – all of that suffuses the poems, even the private ones. For instance, the last poem in the book is called 'The Butchers' and it's an account of Odysseus destroying the suitors when he returns home to Ithaca. Now, one of the roots of that poem is in the kind of tacky, sticky tribal violence which we get in Northern Ireland and, reading through that passage at the end of the *Odyssey*, what I was reminded of was Northern Ireland and a particularly bloody case, the Shankill butchers. So it's about the Shankill butchers and it's about Northern Ireland. Even the poems about the West, the beautiful coast of Mayo, are meant to refract my concern for what's happening at the other end of my island.

There's an earlyish poem of yours called 'The West', which I was reminded of in reading Gorse Fires. *I mean, the title reminds me of 'Western civilisation' as well as 'the west of Ireland'. It seems to me that, in* Gorse Fires, *you are preoccupied with the idea of home – in all senses of the word: from civilisation to Ireland to the house you happen to be living in.*

Yes, one of the themes is home. But not in a cosy sense. Home, as you sense it, when you have a home from home, which is the West of Ireland for me. Home as one senses it reading the *Odyssey*: nostalgia, that marvellous word – which is misused – means the ache for the journey home and really what drives Odysseus is the urge to get home. And home, when I talk to my friend Helen Lewis in Belfast,

who's a survivor of Auschwitz and who talked to me about leaving
the ghetto and looking around with an hour or two to go and thinking: 'What shall I take with me? What bit of home, of my life, will I
take with me?' So it's an enormous concept, 'home', and it's menaced
and threatened wherever one looks.

*It strikes me that some of the violence and cruelty that you're talking
about, which threatens home, seems in those later poems in the book
to come out of home itself. I'm thinking particularly of how Odysseus in 'The Butchers', in order to come home, has to perform these
terrible acts of violence.*

That's one of the terrible ironies that I'm trying to explore in the
book. When the idea of home coincides with an idea of territory,
when there are power struggles within home, that's when the whole
thing can explode dangerously. And it's the corruption which the
search for power brings about that concerns me and the way it
menaces home.

*So this home from home that you're talking about, this natural
world, is it an innocent world?*

I wish it was an innocent world. It's increasingly menaced as well. I
don't quite understand why it's the West of Ireland that I use to
embody my themes. I think a gap in my work is Belfast. I really just
have not written about the city in which I live. Now why that should
be I don't know. Perhaps it's just because I find birds more inspiring
than aeroplanes, and trees and shrubs more inspiring than lamp-
posts and telegraph poles. Perhaps in future work I shall try to write
about the streets of Belfast.

*Your answer implies that it's not so much Belfast as the urban that's
the problem?*

Yes. I hate the term, but I suppose in some ways I'm 'a nature poet'.
Everyone ducks when the notion of nature poetry's mentioned, but
deep down I suspect that cities will disappear. I love looking at holes
in the roads when the workmen are digging up gas-pipes or whatever
and you see the soil that's been buried for generations and realise that
cities are as evanescent as anything else.

*You're implying something about civilisation, aren't you? I think
your poems are ambivalent about the whole meaning of civilisation
– in the sense that civilisation depends on 'the city' and yet somehow
the way we use the word 'civilised' seems to apply much better to the
way we inhabit with birds and flowers.*

Yes, *civis* meaning 'citizen' and I don't think being a citizen comes all that easily to me. When I go to the West of Ireland, I don't go there to have colourful talks with the natives. I go there to look at birds and flowers and the beautiful countryside. I am to some extent a disappointed solitary, a failed hermit. Ultimately, though I would hate to be putting over any glib green message, I think that our relationship with the natural world and with the plants and animals is the major issue now.

Why do you think it is that birds figure so prominently in your poetry?

Well, when I see birds, my heart stops and my stomach churns over. I could rationalise by saying that, as I'm an irreligious man or somebody who doesn't have any formal religion, they're a symbol for me of the human soul, of spiritual aspiration. I was amazed when I read through *Gorse Fires* to realise that practically every poem mentions birds. They obviously go very deep with me and perhaps it's better if I don't ask: 'Why birds?' There they are and I hope they don't fly away.

Talking of birds makes me wonder about your sense of the role of the poet. Obviously in Romantic poetry the bird to some extent stands for the poet and I don't think it would be true to say that that was the case in yours. Nevertheless, one has a feeling in some of your poems of a consciousness of what the poetic role is, sometimes a kind of scepticism. Is that something you think about a great deal?

No, I don't think about it a great deal, but I'm divided in two. Part of me believes that the poet's the shaman, the *musarum sacerdos* – the priest of the Muses: part of me, as well as being a failed hermit, is a failed priest. But then having gone so far I think: 'Come off it – this enterprise doesn't matter at all. It's completely unimportant who reads poetry.' I write poetry because of an inner compulsion. Deep down I believe it's very important, but I think I'm rather shy about saying how important I think it is, not just for me but as an important way for humanity to redeem itself.

London, 23 May 1991
(Broadcast: 3 June 1991)

Peter Scupham

In one of his early poems, Peter Scupham addresses the house he lives in: 'House,' he says,

> I have stuffed you with such lovely nonsense:
> All these sweet things: Clare's poems, Roman glassware,
> A peacock's feather, a handful of weird children...

It's not only a good description of his cavernous old Hertfordshire home, but also of his poems; Scupham is a hoarder of treasures from the past, and it is the past, by and large, that gives the things their sweetness.

Visitors to the house will quickly gather that Scupham also loves *making* things: sometimes things made by hand, such as toys, and the beautiful pamphlets published by his Mandeville Press, which he prints in the cellar; sometimes 'airy nothings', such as amateur theatricals and, of course, poems.

Born in 1933, it was not until he was nearly 40 that Scupham started getting his work published. Since then, though, he has produced as many as eight full-length collections and a *Selected Poems*. His most recent book, published in 1990, was *Watching the Perseids*.

On the face of it you were a late beginner, but I find it hard to believe that someone as prolific as you didn't start writing till his late thirties. How did you start?

I started when I was seventeen or eighteen or so, but then I was not an inventor. I was a *pasticheur*, a parodist, an imitator. The first poems I wrote were translations of Baudelaire, translations of Verlaine, imitations of Browning – that kind of thing. They went in folders. They were a jolly useful training for something later. I actually published a poem I'd written at Cambridge in my first book. It's called 'Vertigo' and it first came out in *Granta*. For some reason I never wrote another one for another ten years or so, although I kept the idea of writing very firmly alive in my mind and had fragments. But I was too busy bringing up four children and teaching in Lincolnshire.

So what finally got you started?

'The hands on the accusing clock / Racing like a torrent round a rock' in the MacNeice poem. The sense that one was always going to do it and one had better start doing it. What actually got me started was one of those ridiculous accidents almost. I wrote a poem and thought 'Well, this is OK' and sent it to Anthony Thwaite at *The Listener* and he took it and, well, that was it really.

The poem that impresses me most of those early poems is a poem called 'The Nondescript', which I believe you wrote for the Friends of the Earth.

It's a slight sort of 'Lake Isle of Innisfree' for me, 'The Nondescript', and was a more mythic kind of poem than I was accustomed to writing at that particular time. It was a poem written under some pressures. It was an environmental poem very much before environmental issues were quite as popular as they are now. The shock of the poem came from the *Torrey Canyon* disaster in the 1960s: going down to Cornwall one year and seeing this huge pall of smoke hanging over the whole of the peninsula, all the gullies and coves crammed with an oily slick and the little fighter planes glinting over the thing as they tried to break the back of the ship, which was broken-backed already on the Seven Sisters reef. This had a kind of impact which I think got through into the poem, which was written very fast.

Do you think that poem is at the root of a lot of what you write?

I think and would hope that it's a poem of suffering and sympathy. I think that suffering and sympathy are things I feel at home with. They come bobbing in and out of all the poems. Very often, in the early poems, the surface glitter, the candy-floss element, somewhat disguised that. But I think that, when I've gone deeply into what I want to write, the sound of someone crying at the back of the universe is a very strong sound – though it's not quite *lachrimae rerum*.

A kind of elegiac feeling?

There *is* an elegiac feeling… 'Elegiac' to me almost conjures up the feeling that the past is the past and remains obstinately so. One of the people I respect most in the poetry of this century is David Jones: the

idea of palimpsests, the idea of overlay, the idea of time being un-
sequential but simultaneous. I think increasingly the poems have
tried to build into their textures some sense of the simultaneity of
death and life. After all, death is simply the continuation of life by
other means and I don't much like the word 'elegiac' if it means laying flowers upon something which is dead and vanished and gone.
No, it's there. It's there: it burns.

*Obviously the past is the main theme of your poetry and your second
book,* Prehistories, *goes a long way back into time, into prehistoric
time, but it also goes back into childhood. History, prehistory and
childhood become very much the same thing.*

Well, I think they do. I think there are elisions all the way through
between myth, history and personal experience. I feel very much that
one can only back into the future and the only thing one can see,
looking forward, is the past – whatever the past is, or all those simultaneous selves and layers which have made one what one is and carry
one, with some buoyancy, sleep-walking backwards into the future.
But I think childhood again is an extremely difficult concept because
of its overlays of nostalgia and my own childhood is not in essence a
nostalgic childhood. It has a great, good place, but it also has an
enormous number of dislocations and terrors.

*Those themes of history and personal memory also come together in
a distinctive way in your next book* The Hinterland, *particularly in
the very elaborate sonnet-sequence that gives its title to the book.
That's an extraordinarily complex poem. What is the structure of it?*

It *seems* extraordinarily complex. It looks like an artificial play, but
then I think truths are contained in artificial plays. The sequence
works by simply taking the last line of each sonnet as the first line of
the subsequent sonnet and then gathering the first lines together to
make a final sonnet, so that out of your normal fourteen-line sonnets
you will build a fifteenth sonnet. It almost looks as if you must start
at the end and work backwards. In fact, curiously enough, I did
nothing of the sort and the whole sequence was written in about
three-and-a-half days – morning, afternoon and evening. I think,
without fudging the issue too much, I felt it as a kind of simultaneity
rather than a sequential thing. But pattern-making comes easily.

*So it wasn't difficult to write? I mean you have a lot of themes to
interlace in that poem.*

The interlacing of the themes comes by sitting on things and squashing them down. For a couple of years before that I'd had certain images from that sequence bobbing through my mind – and certain phrases even, which I kept on murmuring to myself and saying, 'Go down, go down,' rapping them on the head and telling them to come back later when they'd meld with something else. But with complexity of structure in poetry, I sometimes feel that people admire the merest *soupçon* of skill, whereas one takes it for granted that a composer can carry fifteen parts in his head and orchestrate them. A poet who does the same to any considerable extent seems to be regarded as a prodigy he isn't.

Do you think that structure of that sort, particularly highly artificial structure, somehow liberates these thoughts and connections?

Yes, certainly I do. I think the kind of phrases which have always meant something very much to me are 'Rhyme is a fertile source of ideas' and is it Jarrell who says the strength of a genie comes from his being confined in a bottle? I think that's a brilliant remark. Yes, I think so – although I wouldn't like to endlessly make watertight bottles because I think one has to take risks as well.

'The Hinterland' is another poem about your past and it's also about war. War, after The Hinterland, *is something which begins to dominate your poems. Why is that?*

I think it dominates for various and complex reasons. Born in 1933, I belong to that generation with echoes of the Great War still hanging around it: my uncle fought through the First World War; my father-in-law, whose war diaries we discovered long after his death, was of German background and enlisted in the English forces in the First World War. War was the colour and sound and smell of my own childhood: a heady garlic. Peter Levi says somewhere that in wartime everything is coloured by war, whether it's the snail shells in the garden or a tin of food in the pantry. War is a flavour, a garlic, a stink, a smell – a delight too, if one is an honest child. Then I went from that to National Service. So I've never really felt very alien from the sense of war. It's there all the way through. In re-creating my own war years in *The Air Show* I found, like several people of my generation, I was rehaunted by things I thought I'd forgotten coming up with an additional pressure in my late forties and fifties.

You do come across to many people, I think, as a celebrator, as rather an affirmative poet, yet what we've been talking about today has been largely death, loss, war.

Yes, but one has to celebrate the loss and the death as well. One cannot celebrate only what calls out and says: 'I must be celebrated because I'm on the side of light.' One has to celebrate the pair, the dark and the light, and the strength of the darkness makes the light stronger. I've always been a pushover for lights in dark spaces and dark places – candles, fireworks – but the dark, the dark, the dark: that seems still the prevailing thing and the light pushing it away. But even with death – as in the latest book, *Watching the Perseids* – I think a death is not celebrated elegiacally so much as celebrated vividly with the attempt to give a dying person back all those different *personae* in their personality, which can link together and make a one thing. If our condition is to be mortal, to live in a dark place in dark spaces and in a dark time, well then, all one has to do is light stronger candles.

That's why you like the theatre so much presumably?

I like it because of its evanescence, because of its glitter and tat, because of its coming out of nothing and going back to nothing, because of its delight and intensity and then its sudden drift back into ashes again.

And darkness in the wings…

And darkness in the wings. There's always darkness in the wings.

This connects with what is the most obviously celebratory quality in your poetry, which is a love of play of various sorts – of games, toys, artifice, magic.

Yes, I *do* love those things…It's a difficult thing because to love those things can risk simply playing with an assortment of treasures and I don't like my treasures unless they have cobwebs and rough edges to them. But I do like those things very much indeed and I do think that play is a form of knowledge and that the most serious things are best said in terms of play. *Sprezzatura* and *brio* are words I like, as I like 'courtesy' and 'decorum' and a whole host of words which seem to be incredibly valuable nuggets to build seriousness around.

There's an early poem of yours in which a child has a puppet show and is asked how the puppets work. And he says, 'By magic', and then adds, 'By string'. So there's a distinction being made between magic and artifice there. I wonder what you mean by magic exactly?

The indefinable somewhat, the voltage, the *O altitudo*, the sense of gasping, the sense that there is something more which might have been said which can never be said. I always like that (I think) eighteenth-century phrase about beauty having 'an indefinable somewhat'. I think hunting for the 'indefinable somewhat' and trying to put salt on its tail is magic, black magic or white magic.

One of the things about magic which strikes me – and it strikes me even more when I read this rather sombre new book of yours – is the question of to what extent magic means conjuring tricks and to what extent it means the supernatural?

Well, that's an interesting one. It sounds pretentious but I hope I have a sense of the numinous. My gospel on all this would be Auden's 'Making, Knowing and Judging', where he gives his *quicumque vult* and talks about sacred encounters. Those things you must respond to, which are sacred simply because they say, 'Respond, respond, respond' – whether it's a girl dancing or a tramp's feet shuffling on a pavement. That's where the power lies, that's where the 'magic' (which is a curious word) lies.

The new book has much more in it about God and about eternity than the other books…

Ah. What is my faith, you're saying, what is my faith? I don't know. How I wish I did know. One knows what one is moved by. All I can say about that is that my deepest responses always go to where the veils tremble, and my deepest responses in poetry go where the veils tremble. I think of Donne's *Holy Sonnets* and the stunning thing, when my mother died, of my father coming to me at four in the morning and having lain by her – she'd died three hours ago – and coming, creeping to me, saying: 'I need to look something up. I've been lying beside her and I've been going through "And Death Shall Have No Dominion" and various Donne holy sonnets and I need to get this word right.' And I knew beyond doubt what sustaining powers there are in the places where the veils tremble. I think I have some sort of instinct for that, but I don't rationalise.

What about words *though? You seem to have much more trust in words than in almost anything else and your poetry, particularly your earlier poetry, is extremely eloquent and elaborate verbally.*

Oh yes. As Peter Porter once said, he thought he was reading rejected lines from Gray's 'Elegy'! Yes, I've always loved words, but I'm painfully conscious as I get older, too, that elaboration (as many poets have found) is something behind which one wishes to find the plain speech – 'I am a very foolish, fond old man'. But I don't think I could ever part company with the beautiful dandies either: the Wilburs, the Hechts, the John Fullers, the people who make words dance like angels and perhaps sometimes don't seem to say an awful lot with them. There is a dance, there is a music and I'm very responsive to cadence and play, although I'm very passionately concerned to get it to say more than 'I am a game and I dance'.

The new book, being mainly about the deaths of your two parents, avoids this elaboration to some extent. Was that deliberate?

No, it wasn't deliberate as a policy. I think it's probably come out like that. Yes, I think so. One would like to be grave, one would like to be plain, but not quite as plain and as grave as all that. I'd still like there to be a *gamin* streak somewhere.

I recently came across a review which has probably burnt into your soul. It described The Hinterland *(I think) as 'the sort of thing that gives poetry a bad name'.*

Well, perhaps it is. Perhaps poetry ought to have a bad name.

Do you find yourself at all at odds with the poetic climate in this taste for decorum and elaboration?

I should think I am. But there always seem to be a few people around who can manage anything if they can manage it. It's rather a ridiculous thing to say for someone who runs a press and has published a great many poets over the last twenty years or so, but what is going on doesn't interest me – in the sense of it being a jostle, wondering exactly whereabouts one is. I mean, when one thinks of poets like Cecil Day Lewis, who kept on changing their style every few years to try to accommodate themselves to what *might* be possible...I have much more sympathy with Stevie Smith, who when told she wasn't particularly contemporary would say: 'Well the times will just have to enlarge themselves to make room for me, won't they?' I don't think poets should be very good poet-watchers actually. I probably read more prose than poetry.

What prose do you read particularly?

Biographies, letters. I've got a blind eye for fictions. I make them, but I have a blind eye for them and have always got myself clobbered on this business of what is invented and what is so. To cure myself of my inventions I like to read about the Is-ness of Was, so I read people's diaries, autobiographies, memoirs, letters – particularly eighteenth and nineteenth-century ones.

What would you say if somebody accused you of being too pre-occupied with bookish matters?

Well, there are plenty of people who aren't. 'Get stewed: / Books are a load of crap.' Well, they're not actually, are they? I can't help that. I suppose it is an overlay, a hangover in some sense from a bookish family – and yet, curiously, my father's books weren't very real to me when I was young. I did all my serious reading when I was doing National Service and at University read damn little. I grew up in a family where quotations were bandied around; it seemed natural – the *lingua franca* of discourse. I like the sense of the familial, I like the play of quotations. I think it can get to be a nervous tic and I would hope to cut it down a bit. I feel that bookishness is a part of me, but books are also a vehicle for truth and humanity. I can't make an easy distinction between real people and what's in books.

You talk about what you would hope to do, and I wonder if you do have a hope for your poetry. Do you have any aspiration for what you would like to write in the future?

Oh to write a half-way decent poem or two. Can one ask for more? And perhaps not to repeat oneself too much.

London, 13 June 1991
(Broadcast: 1 July 1991)

Ken Smith

Ken Smith is a fertile and various poet, but his work has never developed along smooth, easy or predictable lines. Born in 1938, he first attracted attention in the 1960s, when his first collection, *The Pity*, was published. Like Tony Harrison and Jeffrey Wainwright, he was one of a series of socially committed poets associated with Jon Silkin, the magazine *Stand*, and the English Department at Leeds University. Then, in 1969, he moved to the United States where he published his second book and became for a time, more an American than a British poet.

He returned to Britain in the mid 1970s but remained largely invisible as a poet until his long poem 'Fox Running' broke upon an unsuspecting public. Included in *The Poet Reclining*, his 1982 Selected Poems, this powerful account of a modern wanderer, dislocated and divorced, moving through the streets and tube-lines of contemporary London, established Smith as *the* poet of the urban wilderness. The reputation was reinforced by his next book, *Terra*, and when the position of writer-in-residence at Wormwood Scrubs prison came up in 1985, he must have seemed the obvious choice for it. That experience has given rise to a remarkable prose book called *Inside Time* and more or less dominates two more books of poems.

A new collection, *Tender to the Queen of Spain*, was published in 1993.

You've become a kind of urban bard, but your roots are really in rural England, aren't they?

They were originally, yes. I was born in Yorkshire and I grew up in the country. I went to live in a city when I was about thirteen, which is that fertile time, and I think I first wrote poetry in a reflection of the country. Really it was pastoral that I was looking for and the pastoral, as we know, is a form that comes about when actually the thing has gone. So my roots were there, but of necessity – from living in cities and so on – I've become someone who writes about cities and city life. I realised at some point, some years ago, that I had actually to make myself do that.

The poems in that first book seem almost obsessed with the idea of rootedness and roots. The image of grass dominates the book: grass 'locking the soil in frail roots'. Was it moving to the United States that made you feel uprooted, or were you always uprooted?

I was always uprooted: although we lived in the country, we lived in many different places. My father was a farm labourer and he was always getting the sack, which meant that we were always moving. Every year I went to a different school and kept moving about, so we lived in many different parts of Yorkshire. In fact, my childhood was really quite rootless but it produced the longing for roots, so that here I am – rootless but longing for them.

When you went to America, did that make you feel that there was another perspective, another horizon?

I think it did. I began to feel that, whatever roots we can have, we have to make them portable and carry them around with us. It's like carrying a machine and plugging it into the electricity supply in a different room or a different house. I think I became quite efficient at carrying my own roots with me. Eventually, of course, I wanted to get back and I came back home to England really out of a choice, out of a desire, because I think, in the end, the rootlessness of America and the confusion of it rather got me down.

What form do the roots take when you carry them?

Language, stories, narratives, tales from childhood, family histories – all that kind of thing is what I call 'roots'. Then I think it becomes supplemented by reading history and a knowledge of history and an awareness of what the past consists of. It's that kind of thing.

An element in all those things that you've referred to is the figure of the wanderer, isn't it?

Yes, he recurs again and again in different guises: partly my father, partly myself, partly wanderer figures – Gypsies, tramps, vagabonds, people who wander about, who always attract me and become masks for my own self, for my own work. There's a connection here with Anglo-Saxon literature; it's a conscious evocation of 'The Wanderer' and 'The Seafarer'. I'm very fond of those two poems. I lived

for some years in Exeter and one of my favourite visits was to go to
the Cathedral Library and stare at the Exeter Book. Nowadays you
can't do it – it's inside a fireproof case – but in those days there was
a wonderful librarian who used to let me actually sit there and turn
the pages and copy things out. To actually be able to handle this
book was a wonderful thing. I think those are perhaps my two
favourite poems in the whole language.

Do you think that they shaped your sense of form and rhythm?

Yes, I think so. It's hard to say how, but there's a discursive style that
I think I've adopted from them. I sometimes use that hiatus in the
line, the caesura. I tend to alliterate rather then rhyme. All of these
things come from that Anglo-Saxon origin really.

*When you went to America, something fundamental seemed to
change in your poetry. For example, I notice a change in rhythm,
change in movement, shorter lines perhaps. But the whole method
seems to change. Something pre-rational comes into the poems;
myth, dream, fantasy.*

Yes, all of that. The pre-rational notion is quite interesting. I became
more aware of that. I became less linear, I think, less ordered in the
rather Eng. Lit. way of thinking that I'd had before. I found this vast
country where so many things seem – and quite often are – possible,
that are not really possible in Europe. I also responded to some
American poets – James Wright for instance – poets who seemed to
me to be responding very much to the landscape, and I began to
respond to that same landscape myself. I was consciously thinking of
myth and totem animals and almost a magic world if you like. That
and the world of dreams seemed to me to be as real as the waking
world of daily reality. I decided to pay attention to all that.

*And then, a little before 1980, you wrote 'Fox Running'. That is a
poem about modern England, about Mrs Thatcher's Britain, the
state of modern London and all the rest of it. But it's also a kind of
totemic poem, isn't it?*

Yes, yes, I think so. Because it has a man who is called Fox who iden-
tifies with the animal the fox. The animal the fox has become an
urban animal; it has had to learn to live in a city. And therefore I
identified with this animal that has had to change from rural to urban
surroundings. They don't last very long in cities – foxes – but they
fascinated me in the way that they had adapted to living in cities, and

so I was making an obvious link between the man Fox and the animal that he thinks of in his mind and remembers.

Do you think this totemic way of writing makes your poetry more dramatic than meditative?

More dramatic I think. I would rather have the image than a long discourse. What I try to do is let the images produce the thoughts, but the images have got to be there in the first place.

What about voices?

There are a lot of voices in my work. There are a lot of voices of different people, different wanderers, different masked voices. I like using different voices, I quite like investigating a new voice. What I've been doing lately is just making masks actually: physically making them. Each of these masks, of course, is a different person, a different character, it must have a name, a story. It's actually very fruitful.

Do you write poems for the masks?

I have been doing, yes.

One of the things that strikes a reader about 'Fox Running' and about Terra *is how much they are about a particular sort of urban landscape, a particular sort of England – to the extent that they seem to be a commentary, partly, on the social situation in modern England. Is that something that you would accept: that they are social poems, even perhaps political poems?*

They are certainly social, I think, and in some cases political. Yes. Sometimes they are political statements – statements about unemployment, and about class, and about managerial position and the ruling class and poverty and deprivation. Somewhere I say that 'many people never find the river. / That seems to me like a crime.'

Is there a problem, when you're working through images, in making statements that are politically identifiable?

There can be. There can be. But I don't know that I would want to make a particular political platform statement. I don't particularly belong to or vote for or sympathise with any particular political party and I don't think that I would want to reduce my work down to political slogans. Perhaps they come out as generalisations rather than actual political statements, and I would stress my interest more in the social than the political import of it all.

Do you identify with the oppressed and the weak and the powerless?

With the powerless, I think. The powerless are interesting. I also have an interest in the outsider, because we do not see ourselves, we are inside our own pair of brackets. It needs an outsider to come along and actually point something out. Therefore the wanderer, the Gypsy, the Wandering Jew is always a commentary upon settled and fixed society. That interests me too.

There's a kind of apocalyptic air to some of these recent poems: almost a sort of prophetic feeling about impending disaster. But over against that, there's also another kind of prophecy, which is perhaps utopian or Blakeian. Is that a fair point?

It's a fair point, yes. I'm a great admirer of Blake and a great believer in Blake. My fear about disaster – nuclear disaster or ecological disaster – is fairly well-founded and fairly well shared around the consciousness of the world anyway. Even though we are now apparently in a period of disarmament, it seems that there are a fair number of prophecies of doom coming up. I think Gorbachev said, some years ago, that the really dangerous time is when we actually start to disarm – that's one of the things that we can see in what used to be called Soviet Russia. So I have that fear of impending disaster. In any case, it doesn't seem to me to make sense – we can't go on using the resources of the world to the extent we're using them and hope for them to be still there. And if the East is now going to become capitalist and consumerist, it's going to pollute the planet faster and use up its resources faster, so I don't see too much cause for joy in that either.

In these more recent poems like 'The London Poems' from Terra *and the sequence called 'As It Happens' from* Wormwood *and one or two other things, the preoccupations we've been talking about take on different verse forms. During the American period into 'Fox Running' you had this rather loose, loping, open sort of form. There now seems to be a much greater element of closure in the poems. Where does that come from?*

I'm not really sure where that comes from either. It worries me a bit, because I find myself writing in a much tighter line and a tighter form and everything seems to come out in four line stanzas. I guess I feel comfortable with that, but I'm not exactly happy with it. I rather miss the open, loping form of 'Fox Running' to be truthful.

I'm wondering why it should worry you?

Probably I fear that I'm getting old! That's probably what it is. And tightening up.

Is there some feeling in those poems of working to a fixed form – like a kind of sonnet without the ending on it?

Yes, in fact 'The London Poems', all thirty of them, are three four-line stanzas, which is twelve lines. I've always thought that the interesting part of the sonnet is the first twelve lines and the last two – the couplet at the end – is what sums everything up. I've never been interested very much in the beginning and the end of things. I'm rather interested in the body of things, so I've tended to cut the end off, and I call them – very loosely and only in my own mind – 'loose sonnets'. I'm interested in that form because it does strike me about the sonnet that it is just about the length of a thought that you can have and develop without some outside interference or without extending the thought in another direction. It seems to me an organic and natural thought-form and shape and length.

It must lead to compression, doesn't it?

It leads to compression, yes. I'm trying not to repeat myself too much, I suppose, so the result is compression. It is also the fact that, as a poet gets older, you cannot really go on being lyrical about the sunset and the daffodils and so on, because you've written those poems and it's up to some other young poet to write those poems. Otherwise I think you end up becoming rather fudgy, as Words-worth did.

Just recently your work has been dominated by the experience of working with lifers in Wormwood Scrubs: two books predomin-antly concerned with that subject. I wonder if there's something in prisoners that you identify with, or something about prison that you find emblematic?

I've always been interested in hidden worlds and closed worlds and, going into the world of prison, I discovered this hidden world where so much goes on but nothing is actually known about it outside. It's all like a great big secret, and secrets always interest me. I also, I think, did identify to some degree with prisoners. I felt that the con-dition of imprisonment is something that one could apply to many situations in life, not necessarily institutionalised ones. And cer-tainly, with a lot of the lifers, I used to look at them and think: Well, that could be me quite easily. There are times when I could have mur-dered somebody quite easily in passion. I'm thinking, I suppose, of crimes of passion or crimes that come out of domestic situations or out of love or out of betrayal. I would look at these men and I would think: There's really no difference between you and me except that you *have* killed somebody and you *are* in prison for a long time. But it meant that there were things that they had done that I hoped never to do, which they could actually talk about and tell me about; and that again is a secret world that I wanted to crack open.

On the other hand, you have a sequence of poems called 'Figures in Three Landscapes', which deals with people who committed peculiarly grotesque and horrible crimes. Do you identify with them at all?

Not at all, no. They horrify me and that's why I wrote the poem – in order to try to dispel and contain the horror to some degree.

Is there some connection between the wanderer on the one hand and this contained world of prison on the other?

Well, they stand at quite opposite poles, don't they? The person who's locked up and cannot move and the person who is always on the move and perhaps gets sick of it. That can be a prison too: to be in the prison of the wanderer. It struck me that these two opposite poles of experience were of interest and I began to imagine men who had been outsiders or wanderers and who then are locked up and cannot go anywhere. Very often men would talk about their journeys and their voyages and their wanderings around the face of the earth and they would always be very wistful about it. They would always miss and regret the fact that they couldn't go to the end of the building without permission, or out of the building at all.

You were in Berlin when the wall came down and you wrote a prose book about it; and in The Heart, the Border *there's a handful of poems about Berlin alongside the last of your poems about the Scrubs. Is there a connection for you between the Berlin Wall and the prison wall?*

Yes, quite dramatically and directly. Because having written the *Inside Time* book about prison, I was wandering about in Berlin looking at the Wall and I suddenly realised that I was looking at a great big prison wall and, being able to go through it (as I was privileged to go in and out of the prison) and talking to people on the other side, I thought: They are like prisoners and this is like a prison wall. I then began to see that there was another book I wanted to write about that particular wall and what lay behind it. Of course, that didn't quite happen because the Wall came down as I sat down to write. So I had to change what I was going to write! But that was quite nice because it's being overtaken by history, which always pleases me somewhat!

London, 19 September 1991
(Broadcast: 6 October 1991)

John Peck

In the first poem in John Peck's first book, a party of climbers on a mountain approaches 'the last cols' before the peak:

> Doors in this termless morning
> Sills, thresholds
> And the firmness beyond

It could be a description of Peck's own poems, which are like gateways between consciousness and the world it registers and perceives. His method combines clear definition ('firmness') with what appears to be its opposite – the moment when sensuous experience is transmuted into thought. One is not told what to think. One is invited to re-experience the world.

It is this that makes Peck, for me, the outstanding American poet of his generation – as well as one of the most difficult. He was born in Pittsburgh in 1941. As a young man he went to California to study under Yvor Winters. Then a doctoral thesis on Ezra Pound, which was supervised by Donald Davie, encouraged experimentation. The crisp sensuousness of Chinese poetry, as mediated by Pound's translations, is a key influence on his first two books, *Shagbark* (1972) and *The Broken Blockhouse Wall* (1978). Peck seemed destined for the now familiar career of American academic poet when, in 1984, he embarked on the study of Analytic Psychology at the Jung Institut in Zürich. Since 1993 he has been practising psychotherapy in his native New England. The 1990s have witnessed a spectacular flowering of his talent in two substantial books: *Poems and Translations of Hĭ-Lö* (1991) – Hĭ-Lö is Peck's Chinese heteronym – and *Argura* (1993).

You studied under Yvor Winters at Stanford and then went on to write a doctoral thesis on Ezra Pound under Donald Davie. What would you say to those who argue that Pound and Winters are irreconcilable?

Well, of course one thing to point to is the work of Davie himself. As for Winters, who was both a great and peculiar teacher, he dismissed Pound, to be sure, though not entirely, and not without having paralleled Pound's career in several ways as a younger writer, critic, and publisher. Later on, in part of his trilogy on Theseus, Winters seems to answer Pound's fourth Canto, perhaps the weightiest of the early Cantos to choose for besting. What sets Winters apart is the stand he took against the isolating intensity of mental states which he knew from youth on, and his clear sense of evil, for example in 'A Vision', and then his turn to standard measures after a long experimental phase. But I would guess that a more complex engagement with Pound persisted. Donald Davie's self-renewing colloquy with Pound, from the vantage of an Anglo-Wintersian poetics, certainly suggests that the instigations go on working away. The oxymoronic span of writers now manifestly indebted to E.P. – from Christopher Logue's Homer to Davie, from Peter Dale Scott to Armand Schwerner in *The Tablets* – shows how unsettled Pound's hash remains. Davie is the most interesting because the least obviously indebted at first glance.

Davie, in his essay on Shagbark, *contrasts your emphasis on wood with Pound's on stone. He also praises the elaboration of your syntax in contrast to Pound's more fragmentary manner. Do you recognise this account of yourself?*

I do. Those craftsmanly observations of course carry astute observations about temperament, and Davie has been as sensitive in applying them as was Adrian Stokes in writing on the visual arts and architecture. But since temperament develops, so do some of these ratios. They have changed somewhat with me, although the poems demonstrate that better than I can. Your question prompts some reflections. Our relation to both wood and stone, and therefore to parts of our own nature, is being altered by new materials and technologies, in the same way that our relation to established metres can be altered – enriched and renewed, I think – by more than a century of changes in the modes, to borrow Plato's phrase. These changes are profound; our realignments in the arts are symptoms of them. Pound's elegy throughout *The Cantos* on building and carving in stone, Stokes's writing about these (even the ugly Kleinian parts), and Buckminster Fuller's praise of Pound, are all of a piece – that is, new means and formal values perhaps mean renaissance, but also a reinvestment of our primary imagination in the materials that immemorially carried it in modes now passing away. It is too bad

that Adrian Stokes came to rely on object-relations jargon to express
some of this, but his instincts were trustworthy. We are not abandoning, we are remarrying, wood and stone and the alloys of iron and
steel. Our liminal or transitional position prevents us from seeing the
outcome, but we should not label as nostalgic what instead may
anticipate a redefinition of both our inner ratios and our outer
involvements with materials that have long engaged us *au fond*. This
is a roundabout reply, but one I need in order to side-step the usual
distinctions about syntax. Pound's syntax became marked, even
mannered, by the cantilevered relative clause dangling its verb,
antenna-like, into spaces which seem nostalgic but which function
more gropingly and constructively. That unsettledness or ambivalence is fitting. Though a stone-carver, Pound developed a syntax
which draws to itself analogies other than the chisel. If I take a poem
of my own, the one on our post-von Hofmannsthal, disturbed relation to language, 'By Mummelsee', the first thing I notice is that the
wood-carving in the poem (and I have sometimes been a carpenter)
does not answer directly to your question about syntax. And then,
that a liminal gateway is posted just at the turn of the poem, so that
what is so on one side may not be quite so on the other. Is that true
of the syntax? I notice only that the poem's one short sentence comes
post-gateway, and describes the knife. Where have we gotten?
Perhaps it is time to wash the dishes.

*But the gateway opens up something else. From the first book on you
have images of frames, gateways, porches, thresholds in your poems.
I think of the first poem in your first book, 'Viaticum', the last section
of 'March Elegies', and so on. Are these mediations of reality metaphors for the poem itself?*

Yes, that seems true of them, though without supporting the strictly
reflexive view lately favoured by writers on literature. Your question
makes me realise that these images still touch strong feelings. I'd
guess that such things are held in common. These places offer shield-
ing form but also fluid passages. They provide structure for moments
which are liminal. I believe that dervishes derive their name from
doors. Since these images return in the work, they probably mark
initiations. But they may return, too, because our time asks us to
stand up such points of passage. But timeless matters go with the
images you select – matters that define our human role as frail portals
between worlds. Our great poets make these matters their themes –
Yeats, or Edwin Muir – while prevailing intellectual attitudes continue to turn them aside. Endurance in this human role I've under-

scored in later poems, as with the portal in 'Little Frieze', where under shock the threshold slows passage.

'For one thousand years, for another thousand years...'

Yes, not unlike passage into the borderline inorganic realm in 'Ars Poetica'.

That poem uses a metaphor – crystalline accumulation – that is different from working in wood and stone. Is there some connection between syntax and each of these modes?

Intriguing though this question is, I feel at a loss with it. I am intuitively certain that some such connection, or some suggestion of a connection, pursues each mode, though it may be as subtle as the colouring of tonal keys in music. Rephrasing your question as a general one, I might ask: why does syntax elicit a certain range of master metaphors at a given time? Consider Mandelshtam's rocketing probe of Dante's language, including the syntax, in the *Commedia*. Metaphors are strongly but illuminatingly mixed there. That essay holds more encoded answers to your kind of question than anything else by a modern master.

Are you surprised when readers find you 'difficult'?

Not with respect to what we have just discussed. But in other respects, yes.

You write mostly in free verse now. You also write in the standard metres and in syllabics. But, as with, say, Bunting, your free verse is so tight as to make the term seem a misnomer. Do you scan according to objective principles?

Accentually, in the 'free' zone, which practice taken alone promotes no fineness or differentiation. So, at the same time I plait phonic elements across both accentual and syllabic grids. The results do not submit wholly to rational description, but they draw on processes at work in the poetries of all the major European languages for more than a century. The family resemblances as well as the clan differences in those 'free' traditions would repay study – which one American poet living abroad, Bruce Lawder, has made it his business to pursue. In English, Bunting's ear for these matters spanned the smallest and largest scales. His Celtic visual and Scarlattian keyboard analogies interlace, but that difficulty simply suits the order of complexity which his skill harmonises. Scaling is Pound's domain, plaiting is Bunting's, but those artistries prove to be compatible in

Bunting's hands. We have yet to catch up with him. American poets say they admire him, but they usually don't say why. Their cloudiness may be forgiven, since American habits revolve around the axis of conviction that metrical variation has gone entirely out of the window and that only tone, and tones of voice, have moved in to replace it. A titration of one of Eliot's impulses, but diluted beyond recognition.

Is your metrical pluralism provisional or principled with respect to those habits?

May I cross a Pauline reply – what I do is not what I may intend to do – with the observation that the innovations of Sir Thomas Wyatt, were they floated today, would go unperceived? Let me interject a different observation: that because of linguistic experiment from surrealism to Stein's recombinatory probes and onward, the life that we may find in strophic and stanzaic composition, the older syntaxes of thought-rhythm (and somatic under-thought), ought to seem more interesting, yet usually goes unexamined by both its upholders and its spurners. That is odd, since the older patterns are resonance fields no less than are the new ones. Our social and class feelings about all of these patterns carry great weight, as they must. Yet those associations cannot account entirely for the capacity a given pattern has for resonance. Perhaps I should say, rather than the new life *in*, the new perceptions *of*, established patterns alongside fledgling ones – a virtuoso of Schoenberg may turn back to Brahms with altered ears, hearing Brahms anew without compromising artistic and social conscience. Which chance it would be sad to miss, since all of our patternings, old and new, function in ways that we understand as poorly as we do the holistic generation of form in nature.

Between The Broken Blockhouse Wall *and* Poems and Translations of Hi-Lö, *there's a gap of twelve years. Then almost immediately* Argura *follows. What happened in that gap?*

The transitions to Europe, new training, and freelance work preoccupied me, as did a requisite interval of purgatory. Some poems in both books antedate that time; the rest slowly came later or filled out the idea for each book once it stood clear.

Has Analytical Psychology affected you as a poet? Has it, or has Jung, influenced your poetry?

No doubt, in ways that I would be the last to see. But Jung's psychology has deepened my respect for the gap between framing an intuition in words and actually taking in what the larger personality would have one incorporate. The actual effort may require many years. It has also let me see more clearly the writer's burden of inhabiting two worlds at once. And see that though this be the case, whatever gifts come in over the transom should not be greeted naively or super-stitiously.

What would you say to those poets who suspect that to psychologise themselves would be to kill the goose that laid the golden egg?

That they are being proprietary about the gold and too dainty about the goose. If they are resisting the mechanistic and personalistic cartoons that usually pass for psychology, well and good. The jargons of psychology, at least in the American setting, serve as questionable surrogates for all that is missing in our atomistic and barbaric disregard for a public realm. But it is also the case, and a humbling case it is, that poetic work, or imagination and the labours consequent on it, is only one instance of our relation to autonomous psychic processes that go on out of sight continuously, with which we may cohabit but never master, but which (as imagination in a comprehensive sense) can be somewhat altered very slowly, just as a poem can be altered more quickly, by our attention to them. Perhaps this is in part what Yeats did in writing *A Vision*. So, protective diffidence and sly arrogance on our part about that order of fact is ill-advised. In holding such attitudes, we also disregard what Jackson Knight infers about the way in which Virgil worked, or what we know about how Mandelshtam worked. 'Courting the Muse' remains a quaint figure only to the innocent.

Hĭ-Lö is Chinese. There are 'Chinese poems', though, as early as the Colophons in Shagbark. *How did you first get interested in Chinese poetry?*

Through Pound's work at first, and then A.C. Graham, and the work of Bernhard Karlgren and other scholars.

Can you read Chinese at all? Where did Hĭ-Lö come from and how did he come about?

Not without crutches, or over the shoulders of emigrés and scholar-friends. Hĭ-Lö inverts Li Ho, on whom I worked much earlier with the help of Mrs Susan So. He came to life through my own exile's eyes, at first playfully, as a way of conjuring with impressions.

Can we talk about translation? Hĭ-Lö, the book, is in two halves:
Hĭ-Lö's 'own' poems, and his translations of various foreign poems
into English – though it's English filtered through a sort of Chinese
mind-set. Are the poems in the first half also, in a sense, translations?
Are they not linguistic but cultural translations, not unlike the sub-
ject rhymes in Pound?

The idea is that of the *roman à clef*, but with the atmosphere of an
era, rather than a biography, as the subject. Since my circumstances
were those of an exile, though usually not straitened ones, you might
say that the poet was translated before his poems were. 'Cultural
translations' I will accept, though that may aggrandise what was
sometimes playful or wicked, though certainly *plotted* under the
terms you have in mind. My interest, too, was in touching registers
on the *whole* of the keyboard available to us, at the risk of occasionally striking a vulgar note. The sheer amount of literary translation
done now lifts plumes of industrial smoke into the air, with incalcul-
able effects. I take a poke at that fact while also indulging the practice
to an end. To be sure, in some cases I stand on several sets of shoulders in order to do so. Occasionally the effort is both experimental
and scrupulous, as in the version of Wang Wei, where I hazard a cor-
relative for the musical tones borne by Chinese characters, or in the
poems derived from Karlgren's inventorial readings of archaic
inscriptions.

Argura must have been written over many years, but it reads like a
single project, as the very pregnant title suggests. Was it? What does
'Argura' mean?

Yes, it was. And the title, as anagrams do, means what combinations
and root-talk mean. The diamonds between the majuscules* are not
the currently fashionable designer's sprinkles, but a Roman inscrip-
tional convention, signalling here that the elements should go into
recombination. Argument, and augury, but other possibilities as
well, which canvass the book's themes. The title is a gift from the
unconscious, arriving at the end of a search and only then yielding to
scrutiny.

You are very preoccupied with form in nature and form in art – and
with their relation. I think of the frequently recurring formations of
birds echoing human and aesthetic formations, as in the wonderful

---

* This is how the title appears on cover and title page. [CW]

'Migration', for instance, or in 'Passacaglias'. This seems connected with the preference for argumentum *over* ratio...

Yes, it is connected, since the arguable is both proposed and to some extent given, with respect due to the given. But it is easy to be misunderstood here, since modernist work has already achieved its corrective, through Joyce's Aquinian 'modality of the visible', Dr Williams's things, Pound's natural object, Oppen's 'this in which', even Cunningham's haeceity. Held to, this view grows one-sided, blinkering itself to those *realia* which are not visible, to which both Yeats and Pound, after all, paid assiduous attention whether in Stone Cottage or out of it. I do not mean that Robert Duncan's Coleridgean, quasi-neoplatonic volubility is to be preferred, but only that reality in its fulness is going to insist on poking in. One way of rendering the cosmogonic beginning of John's gospel would be to say, 'Energy is already patterned and forever patterning'. The craftsman's emphasis may fall either on seeing the result – actually seeing things, or seeing and loving persons, is hard – or on acknowledging the ways in which energies turn into things and persons and then pass away – incarnation is after all an agony aimed at a transformation.

Incarnation is also Christian and not Chinese. Are you specifying something about these relations of form?

But neither is incarnation specifically Greek and Christian, as Simone Weil underlined for herself in turning to the Vedas. To restrict this to art: tradition is neither ideal nor an idea but incarnate (an aphorism by the painter Fairfield Porter), and the heritage is not passed on but conquered (that's Malraux). Those two viewpoints, feminine and masculine, give a whole picture.

Well, increasingly your emphasis seems to be on history and what we inherit from the past. My favourite of all your poems is 'He who called blood builder', which draws on the Aeneid, *itself a great meditation on history and heritage. Your ambivalence is Virgilian, though it also reminds me of Geoffrey Hill. But when I discussed this with Robert Wells, he suggested that you were more resigned to the ambivalence than Hill is, more willing to accept a tainted (but not a poisoned) chalice, maybe nearer to being optimistic. Would you agree with that assessment?*

Yes. A short-term pessimist often holds fast to the radiant rag of hope. 'Frieze from the Gardens of Copenhagen' speaks to this. Our well-informed glooms may draw on only part of our nature, and on those forms of feeling that preoccupy us *en masse*. As for the Virgilian, there is already of course the poetry of Allen Tate, perhaps along with John Crowe Ransom one of Geoffrey Hill's exemplars. But passion more than ambivalence informs Tate's Virgilian feelings. A poem as darkly magnificent as 'The Subway' (not one of the explicitly Virgilian poems) evokes for me an opposite number, George Oppen's 'Vulcan', on the same subject. Both poems strive to contain adult anger by reference to pre-adult revery, neither mental state being sufficient alone to span the accelerated malformations of our 'built environment', as the planners now blandly call it. And that spanning cannot quite be managed with Virgilian ambivalence, whether it be felt on the Left or Right side of one's grip.

I find your poetry unlike almost anything else that's being written at the moment and wonder if that's not why it's still insufficiently recognised. For instance, you seem wholly uninterested in 'the self', which is not exactly fashionable – and you're not post-modernly reflexive either. This is perhaps surprising in a psychologist. Do you feel at home in the current climate?

No, but for whomever that is the case, it still leaves them in good company. As for the wide currency of memoir and *verismo* family sentiment, these prevail, touchingly, in societies whose continuities break and whose personal bonds shatter under systemic pressures. Then, too, popular conceptions of 'the self', even the ones prevailing in literary discussion, however brightly lit and congested the notions may be, are passing and fluid next to the Self upper-case, however we choose to name it (*Atman* is an ancient term, which Jung expressed humility in borrowing). Among poets, Yeats again would be one who stands over against much current feeling. Already in the 1960s George Oppen curtly rejected these still-preferred currencies, saying (I approximate): 'The miracle is not that we have a self, the miracle is that we have something to stand on'. Of course, his viewpoint was politically engaged, thoroughly masculine, and typically American in its wondering preoccupation with the external world. But there is more to the world, and it is intriguing that the fluid syntax of Oppen's later poetry turns towards it. But the truism that we share a self with others compels recognitions which not only George Oppen would underscore. The facts of general assault on the planet and the political slaughter of innocents seep constantly into awareness. Conscious innocent action perceives its own participation by default, and is forced to inquire into that scandal. The reflection of action which poetry is – I leave that vexed question hanging – will inevitably reflect these matters somehow. Were we to adapt David Jones's Welsh inscription – 'The bards of the world assess the men of valour' – from epic tones to contemporary ones, I wonder what we might hear, or overhear, in it?

Brattleboro, Vermont,
October – December 1993

Ted Hughes

Some thirty years ago, in one of the poems for which he is still best known, Ted Hughes recalled himself as a boy fishing for pike in the South Yorkshire countryside. As night falls, he comes into contact with forces so deeply rooted in the scene and in the human psyche, that recorded history seems to evaporate. 'Stilled legendary depth,' he says of the pond, 'It was as deep as England.'

When Hughes became Poet Laureate in 1984, a good many readers expressed surprise. Yet as those lines indicate, he has always had a feeling for nationhood, though often a disturbing and uncompromising one. Now, with the publication of his book of Laureate poems, *Rain-Charm for the Duchy*, we have the chance to examine his interpretation of this public role.

We have also seen him recently in another role that is new to him – as interpreter of our greatest national poet. His *Shakespeare and the Goddess of Complete Being* is a massive work, perhaps more mythography than criticism, which sees the whole of Shakespeare's mature work as a development of two fundamental myths, first explored in the long poems, *Venus and Adonis* and *Lucrece*.

At 61, Hughes remains very productive – he is also, for instance, an important children's author – and he lives on a small farm near the northern edge of Dartmoor, where I went to interview him.

When did Shakespeare first grip your imagination?

Well, it's ridiculous to say it, but I was interested in Shakespeare long before I was interested in literature or poetry. I think because he was simply a legendary figure. I can remember my father...I doubt if he had ever sat down to read Shakespeare – he might have heard the odd line drifting around – but he had these intimate anecdotes about him, such as that 'When Shakespeare read a newspaper, he could remember every word of it!' And so he became an interesting figure. My mother bought a whole set of the plays when I was quite young. I can remember going through these *Warwick Shakespeares* – they were that edition. I suppose then the next step was reading *King Lear* for Higher School Certificate. I was then sixteen. Around that time I knew *Macbeth*, I pretty well knew *King Lear*, and I knew most of *Antony and Cleopatra*: I was constantly trying to learn them. So I was deeply riveted.

Your new book on Shakespeare is basically concerned with two myths you find at the root of his work – myths of the Great Goddess and the sacrificial god – and I know you've always been interested, since you were very young, in myth and folklore, but I feel this doesn't really surface in your work until quite late, till about your third book, Wodwo, *and then most inescapably in* Crow. *I wonder if you can say how that change came about?*

Looking back now at my first books, I can trace odd leading images directly back to certain mythical things that interested me. For instance, the 'Hawk Roosting'. He's a straight monologue for a notion of the Egyptian hawk, Horus: the immortal hawk who is the eye of the sun, who flies through all hawks, or who absorbs all hawks. In a sense I was trying to raise the creatures that I'd encountered in my boyhood in South Yorkshire and West Yorkshire. I was trying to raise them into some mythic frieze. I was thinking of them as a sort of mural. The pike, for instance: they were to be angels hanging in the aura of the Creator. So they were just hanging there in the great ball of light, just pulsing away there, very still. That's why they're so still, because they were originally angels. My model, I remember, was Blake's 'Tyger'. I was thinking, if I could raise my pike to that kind of intensity and generality! That was the ideal. There were much more obvious efforts to do that in the original draft, but I cut them out and left myself with the old South Yorkshire fish. But that was the original purpose and motivation behind the poem itself, and so too with the hawk. So too with some others.

It seems to me that there's a curious kind of impatience in your work with what you might call the props of civilisation: with habits of rational thought and with decorum. Do you feel that you're, in your poetry, trying to bypass those habits of thought to get back to some earlier stage that antecedes them?

Well, I'm not sure that's right. My approach to that dilemma was in a way from the inside. For instance, at university, the literary criticism that was then developing...It was just in its early days, in its

Leavis days. I was very curious in it and I had my talents for perform-
ing in that way – I quite enjoyed it. But I could see also that it had
some quite devastating effect on whatever it was in me that wrote.
Certain types of thought, certain attitudes – I'm aware of them not
as something alien, nor as something wrong, but as something that
is destructive to something else in me. I have my share of rationality,
but I know, for instance, that when I indulge it...in other words,
when at university I used to try and write critical essays, I simultaneously suffered that process as some sort of terrible damage to
myself. And this wasn't just a fancy idea; it presented itself to me in
quite vivid dreams, which were extremely disturbing – they were a
sort of breakdown, I suppose. They were strong enough to determine
my abandoning English as a degree course. I felt I just couldn't continue with that. And it also decided my not teaching. I very much like
teaching but, at the same time, I realised that, if I wanted to hang on
to whatever it was that made me write at all, I couldn't indulge
myself. I can see that other people can: other people can manage it
without problem. It's obviously something that's peculiar to me – or
perhaps shared by others who have a make-up like me.

*But given that it is such a sensitive instrument, it might seem to many
people surprising that you've been willing, recently, to take on a very
public role as a poet: to be Poet Laureate. One might reasonably
have thought that you were not the kind of writer who would write
occasional poems to much effect. Yet I think a lot of people agree
that many of them have been surprisingly effective. I think particularly of the poem called 'Rain-Charm for the Duchy'. How do you
feel about that?*

I'm more than a monarchist in that I've always had the belief that the
symbol of royalty is an essential expression of psychological unity,
psychological wholeness, so that just a single figure, living in a single-
figure world, would come up with the dream of royalty as the centre
of the whole psychological complex, the whole ordering of whatever
it is that emerges from our biological make-up, when it's unified and
when it's ordered and when it's intact within itself. If it is aware of its
deepest centre, it is aware of that deepest centre as something
perhaps to which you begin to give divine names, and at the point
where those divine qualities, or what we call divine qualities, become
ordinary human qualities, somewhere at that point you have an
intermediary figure, who has always been called a king or a queen.
That's how, presumably, these figures were invented. They didn't
impose themselves. They came out of the dreams of ordinary people,

they were crowned by the dreams of little bunches of primitive tribes-men and by the dreams of big nations. So in that way I look on it as a centre, and an essential centre, in a community. And I think when you take that idea of divinity out of the centre, when you pluck it out as if you pulled the axis out of it and you say, 'We're having no truck with any of this divinity rubbish – we're just secular, independent, objective, rational men, dealing with the problems as they come up,' what you've actually done is pull out the root that draws up the ener-gies into your ordinary personality from whatever is beneath your ordinary personality. In other words, I think you've pulled out the essential thing that keeps the self and the community whole. So my feeling about writing about this figure, this idea of royalty, is not a strange one to me. It's an opportunity to say something that I really believe.

So that the poems are something more than occasional really...

To me they are, yes.

In the 1970s you did some work for the theatre with Peter Brook – your version of Seneca's Oedipus, *and a play called* Orghast *for which you wrote a whole new language. How much did you learn from that experience?*

When I first worked on that particular project with Peter, he was put-ting together a play for the Shiraz Festival. He had his international company of actors – all different languages. He assumed that the audience in Persia would be international or would be Iranian. The drift of his whole experiment at that time was to search for a kind of theatre, or rather a kind of acting, which would communicate to all human beings in that it wouldn't have the divisiveness of being characterised by a single culture or a single language. So in a sense that meant the actions had to be not necessarily primitive but cer-tainly very generalised, sort of mythical I suppose or at a folklore-mythical level. And to begin with we had no language at all. We were just using bird-cries. We were hoping to force the actors back into resources behind verbal expressiveness, back into some sort of musical or other kind of expressiveness. And in the course of this I wrote one scene about the vulture visiting Prometheus on his crag. I wanted to write a text of some kind so that I could organise the music of it. So I just invented about half-a-dozen words and automatically – because you don't want to invent meaningless sounds – I made each syllable represent what I considered to be one of the central ideas of the drama. I found from that that you could develop quite a large vocabulary, making different combinations of the root-syllables, and eventually I did develop an enormous vocabulary. Then automatically I began to introduce a grammar: I began to introduce cases, tenses – the whole thing just automatically turned into a language. And it wasn't as though I were thinking it out with great labour; it just automatically evolved in that way – on the pattern, I suppose, of Latin and so on, though it felt like instinct. But as it became a language, it began to work less and less well with the actors because, as it became a language, they began too to consider it as a language, they began to use it as a language in the scenes, so, instead of driving them right back into the absolute last-ditch efforts to express something or other that couldn't be expressed in words, they were simply talking, just using my language as ordinary language. It was more like Chekhov and we wanted something like the first Parliament of the Apes. So then I broke it all down again, simplified it all, invented in a way a new language. And after that I didn't tell the actors what the words meant. And that began to work again then. So it was a double experiment really. It was first of all the experiment discovering how easy it is to make a language, how natural it is to make a language; and then how, as the language became full of verbal meanings, it ceased to draw on any of the expressive resources of the people using it. They simply then used it as a code, putting less and less and less expressiveness into it – hiding behind it more and more. To get them to reveal themselves again, we had to destroy that language and give them again a sequence of cries which had no verbal meaning. Then once again they were forced back onto other resources and tremendous, exciting, strange, musical things could happen again. That was interesting.

Does that actually affect the way you write poetry?

I think it sharpened my sense of the mosaic quality of verse. I was already very, very aware of it because, for instance, Sylvia's poetry seems to me, almost in a unique way, a mosaic kind of patterning of almost separate, distinctive units of meaning. Obviously words always are distinctive units of meaning, but in her world they're particularly graphically arranged: each unit has a distinctive individuality of its own and is very pointedly contrasted and related to all the others around it, which is part of its beauty and its strength. So I was very aware of that. But actually, my experience with Peter enormously strengthened that sense of the way verse does operate. When language begins to operate like that, one's attention or the meaning is somehow pitched beyond the superficial syntactical meaning.

You've been working down here as a farmer for some time, and you've always been passionately concerned about the condition of nature. Do you feel moved as a poet to use your art to bring environmental issues to people's attention?

Well, I think it would be nice if you thought you could. But, if you are concerned about these issues and you've had much experience with actually trying to do something about them, you realise that most efforts don't work. In fact, most efforts on most levels achieve the opposite: they somehow immunise the status quo against change, against becoming more anxious about these issues. I should say for myself that I'd feel, writing a poem about any particular issue of this kind, that I were doing about the weakest thing I could do to help it – unless it earned some cash that could be donated.

Nevertheless, one of the themes that comes across most powerfully from your poetry from first to last is the theme of survival and I wonder if you feel at all, in spite of the moments of pessimism, that poetry is primarily something which brings hope?

For myself, I formulated a little notion that art is in general the psychological component of the immune system. As the body tries to heal itself from any stress or shock or infection, the corresponding harmonic in consciousness is art. And so our constant struggle to pull ourselves together and to deal with difficulty and with injury and with illness and with threats and fears manifests itself at the psychological level as art. We may not think at the moment it's the most valuable thing we do, but of any past civilisation the one thing that we want to preserve is their art. Because it still operates for us as medicine.

North Tawton, Devon, 23 March 1992
(Broadcast: 5 April 1992)

Index

Fenton, James ix, 36-42
Fitzgerald, Robert 24
Freud, Sigmund 19, 92
Frost, Robert 81
Fry, Christopher 98
Fuller, John 126
Fuller, R. Buckminster 137

Garibaldi, Giuseppe 25
Gautier, Théophile 25
Geldof, Bob 76
Geoffrey of Monmouth 93
Gershon, Karen 67
Goethe, J.W. von 98
Gömöri, George 43
Goya, Francisco de 108
Graham, A.C. 141
Graves, Robert 31, 65, 92
Gray, Thomas 102, 125
Greene, Graham 25
Grigson, Geoffrey 87, 88
Gunn, Thom vii, ix, xi, 1-7, 70
Gurney, Ivor 83, 87, 88
Guthrie, W.K.C. 95

Hall, Sir Peter 98
Hardy, Thomas 52, 54, 117
Harrison, Tony ix, xi, 97-103, 128
Havel, Václav 47
Heaney, Seamus ix, 77-82, 113, 114, 116
Heath-Stubbs, John ix, xi, 90-96
Hecht, Anthony 126
Herbert, George 10, 11
Herbert, Zbigniew 82
Hesiod 108
Hill, Geoffrey ix, 143, 144
Hitler, Adolf 64
Hobsbaum, Philip 113
Hofmannsthal, Hugo von 138

Holub, Miroslav 82
Homer 85, 108, 137
Hooker, Jeremy ix
Hope, A.D. 104
Hopkins, G.M. 58, 59, 60, 72, 82, 105
Horace 8
Hughes, Ted vii, xi, 71, 146-151

Isherwood, Christopher 4

Jackley, Nat 98
Janáček, Leoš 117
Janmaat, Anna xii
Jarrell, Randall 123
Jeffers, Robinson 18, 19
Jennings, Elizabeth ix
Johnson, Samuel 8
Jones, David 121, 145
Joyce, James 71, 93
József, Attila 43
Jung, C.G. 19, 92, 144

Kádár, János 44
Karlgren, Bernhard 141, 142
Kavanagh, P.J. 83-89
Keats, John 29, 82, 93, 96
Keyes, Sidney 92
Klein, Melanie 137
Kleinzahler, August ix, 6, 7
Knight, W.F. Jackson 141
Kundera, Milan 47

Laforgue, Jules 25
Larkin, Philip 7, 26, 30, 70
Lawder, Bruce 139
Lear, Edward 36
Leavis, F.R. 148
Lehmann, John 64
Levi, Peter 123
Lewis, C. Day 64, 126